RISING TO THE CHALLENGE

CHALLENGE

Lessons Learned From
Guilford Technical Community College

Edited by John E. Roueche and Suanne D. Roueche

RISING TO THE CHALLENGE

Lessons Learned From
Guilford Technical Community College

Edited by John E. Roueche and Suanne D. Roueche

Community College Press®
A division of the American Association of Community Colleges
Washington, DC

Suggested citation:

Roueche, J. E., & Roueche, S. D. (Eds.). (2012). *Rising to the challenge: Lessons Learned From Guilford Technical Community College*. Washington, DC: Community College Press.

Community College Press® is a division of the American Association of Community Colleges (AACC), the primary advocacy organization for the nation's community colleges. The association represents more than 1,200 two-year, associate degree–granting institutions and more than 13 million students. AACC promotes community colleges through five strategic action areas: recognition and advocacy for community colleges; student access, learning, and success; community college leadership development; economic and workforce development; and global and intercultural education. Information about AACC and community colleges may be found at www.aacc.nche.edu.

On the Cover: The H5 high-rise building on the Guilford Technical Community College (GTCC) High Point Campus, North Carolina. GTCC offers a diverse mixture of curriculum, continuing education, and developmental education courses. Entertainment technology, human services, pharmacy technology, and simulation and gaming are the signature programs at this campus. Photo by April N. Wright.

Design: Brian Gallagher Design
Printing: Global Printing

Library of Congress Cataloging-in-Publication Data

Rising to the challenge : lessons learned from Guilford Technical Community College / Edited by John E. Roueche and Suanne D. Roueche.
        pages cm
        Includes bibliographical references and index.
        Summary: "Presents measures taken at Guilford Technical Community College to ensure student and institutional success in the face of economic, accountability, and completion challenges. GTCC's experience serves as a model for any community college facing the same challenges"—Provided by publisher.
        ISBN 978-0-87117-395-9 (alk. paper)
        1. Guilford Technical Community College. 2. Academic achievement—North Carolina—Guilford County. I. Roueche, John E. II. Roueche, Suanne D.

LD6501.G85R57 2012
378.756'62—dc23

2012010640

Printed in the United States of America.
First Edition, First Printing

CONTENTS

FOREWORD

Resourcefulness and an entrepreneurial spirit have been hallmarks of the community college since its inception more than a century ago. This institutional model is, after all, a uniquely American invention within the more traditional higher education community, created to embody and advance democratic values of open access and equal opportunity to learning.

Over their substantial and distinguished careers, John and Suanne Roueche have been at the forefront of educators who have made understanding and celebrating the community college a singular focus. In an extraordinary body of work that includes books, articles, lectures, and iconic professional development programs, they have analyzed and engaged community colleges and helped to advance their leaders. From that rich foundation of work, they have written insightfully and inspiringly about the qualities that make some colleges exceptional and worthy of emulation—from *Embracing the Tiger: The Effectiveness Debate and the Community College,* to *The Entrepreneurial Community College,* to *The Creative Community College,* and more.

Now in this new work, the editors, along with contributing authors Martha Ellis and Melinda Valdez-Ellis, turn their astute lens to the future. Through that prism, they focus on what they describe as the "dichotomy that exists between funding decline and enrollment growth," two stark realities that colleges must not only cope with in the present but that are also likely to become more pronounced in coming decades. The challenge of doing more with less is already far too familiar to most community colleges. But the colleges—and indeed, the nation—have substantially more at risk in a knowledge society where demographic change is rapid and profound.

As institutions with the broadest mission and the most diverse student population in higher education, community colleges are affected in unparalleled ways by the shifts in our social and economic framework. Many college leaders are already confronting these challenges in strategic and innovative ways. However, one college, the authors believe, represents a distillation of new ways of operating that will redefine the community college of the future: Guilford Technical and Community College (GTCC). In this compelling and carefully documented narrative, the authors address an intriguing question: "How would a college that started as a small, rural training center grow to become a major player on a regional, state, national, and international stage?"

The operational emphasis of this book is progressive and forward looking, underscoring the importance of forging strategic alliances, leveraging technology, and making performance-based decisions. But the authors also examine a fundamental aspect of the learning enterprise that is, has been, and will forever remain central to success: strong, consistent, and transformational leadership. Until his retirement in 2011, former GTCC President Don Cameron led the college for more than a decade, a longevity factor that studies indicate contributes significantly to evolutionary and transformational change. His leadership attributes—a clearly articulated vision, a willingness to take risk, consensus building, and strategic goal-setting—represent competencies that empower others and inspire commitment.

Thus *Rising to the Challenge: Lessons Learned From Guilford Technical Community College* goes far beyond showcasing the dynamic growth and success achieved by one college and one leader. Instead, it articulates enduring and demonstrated principles that can guide any college to loftier goals, greater achievement, and sustained excellence.

Walter G. Bumphus
President and CEO
American Association of Community Colleges

PREFACE

How would a college that started as a small, rural training center grow to become a major player on a regional, state, national, and international stage? This book highlights one such college, Guilford Technical Community College (GTCC) in North Carolina. Although GTCC is certainly not the only community college that has been successful, we believe it provides a helpful example for current and future college leaders. This book examines the approach GTCC has taken and the impact a long-term president was able to have, navigating risk and opportunity to build programs and relationships that helped the college achieve its goals. Fortune, circumstances, and teamwork all contribute to a college's success, but leadership brings these forces together.

We believe there is value in analyzing the way GTCC has achieved a reputation for living in and for its community at a high level of service, quality, and success. GTCC offers best practices worthy of consideration for adoption or adaptation elsewhere—best practices in leadership, stewardship, partnerships, and teaching and learning that demonstrate high performance and achievement standards. In this book, we describe some of the GTCC initiatives, programs, and success stories.

The introduction discusses the backdrop against which all community colleges must operate, as colleges are asked to provide more services to support their communities even as funding sources continue to decline. Chapter 1 focuses on leadership, highlighting GTCC's example of "transformational" leadership that has met challenges in creative ways to effect change. Chapter 2 highlights GTCC's strategies for developing committed leaders from within the college to succeed those who are retiring. Chapter 3 discusses GTCC's approach to pursuing student success and striving to maintain the college's "open door." Chapter 4 describes GTCC's efforts to support student success early by building relationships with the preschool-through-college (P–16) pipeline. Chapter 5 discusses GTCC's collaboration with local industry to ensure economic stability for the college as well as the community it supports. Chapter 6 presents GTCC's innovative establishment of the Larry Gatlin School of Entertainment Technology.

WHY THE FOCUS ON GUILFORD TECHNICAL COMMUNITY COLLEGE?

We have studied many community colleges with extraordinary programs and initiatives that continue to flourish despite today's financial and service challenges. We have documented a wide array of strategies being implemented at colleges that have reputations for being creative, entrepreneurial, and successful partners. The colleges have addressed access, success, and achievement for students and have been instrumental in changing the lives of the citizens of the communities they serve. These colleges showcase adoptable, adaptable models that peer colleges have chosen to implement, often sparking new, unique ideas.

The more we studied community colleges, the more curious we became about the prevailing notion that they should just continue to work at what they know and have proved they can do well and not take the chance of diluting or weakening currently strong programs by creating a plethora of others. Our major thesis was that, traditionally, many community colleges have hesitated to argue with the idea that they cannot offer a wide range of programs to a diverse student population while maintaining a significant number of them at high-performance levels. However, numerous 4-year universities with national reputations and rankings across a broad spectrum of colleges, disciplines, and programs have succeeded in providing an extraordinary number of curriculum offerings to a remarkable number of constituencies. We began to wonder whether community colleges were stepping away from an idea they should embrace.

We wondered if major successes in some areas of the college would necessarily set significant limits on the number of successes that could be supported across the curricular spectrum. Moreover, we began to consider how the negative economic realities of the last decade or so might have encouraged colleges that would not have bought into that idea in better times to be more inclined to buy into it now. Our discussions led us to focus on studying those colleges that appeared to be defying the odds.

We decided to examine colleges that had "all of their burners turned up high and their pots boiling," and there were many from which to choose. We were amazed and comforted at finding many colleges expanding existing programs, establishing new ones, and seeking out funding opportunities during a time when some colleges defined the current economic situation by limited choices and commitments to do the best they could with what they currently had.

Our overarching goal was to inform practice by looking at what very successful colleges were doing, why they did it, how they did it, who was involved, what they gained (or lost) in the process, and what happened as a result. We started with the following common criteria:

- Program diversity.
- Student success agenda.
- P–16 initiatives.

- People development and succession planning.
- Community and economic development.
- Utilization of current technologies.
- Strategic alliances, collaborative efforts, and partnerships.
- Innovation.
- Recognition at local, state, national, and international levels.

We then identified colleges with documentable success across the landscape of this list—the more touch points, the more potential for informing practice. We then narrowed the search with two additional criteria:

- Existence of detailed historical information about the college's people and pursuits.
- Consistent leadership of a single president over a historically significant period of time.

We were aware of GTCC's P–16 program and initially intended to study that program alone as a separate effort. As we got to know GTCC, however, we realized it offered best practices in many other areas. Realistically, we needed to narrow our choice to one college that we could study in depth, and GTCC met the selection criteria exceptionally well.

Located in a large urban county in North Carolina that includes two of the state's largest cities—Greensboro and High Point—GTCC is the third-largest community college in the North Carolina Community College System, with four campus locations. During the college's 50th anniversary in 2008, president Donald W. Cameron, who served from 1990 to 2011, commissioned the book *Guilford Technical Community College 1958–2008: Creating Entrepreneurial Partnerships for Workforce Preparedness*, by Lee W. Kinard, Jr. (2008). Kinard worked for the college in the area of economic development and earlier as executive assistant to the GTCC president following a career as a television anchor and radio host. Kinard's book provides a detailed account of the college's evolution from industrial training center to comprehensive community college, complete with, as he describes, "controversy, lamentations, trials, and tribulations," personalities, events, and outcomes. The book tells a story of patience and persistence as GTCC responded to an array of challenges through its leadership and its programs. Kinard's book makes clear that there is value in colleges' documenting the detailed histories of their achievements. We relied on Kinard's history to provide context for this book, as we sought to take a deeper look at some of the programs and topics.

Cameron retired in 2011, but we include many examples of his leadership decisions and style because we believe his unusual longevity as president had a profound influence on the college's path. As one testament, the college trustees have named the college's new Northwest site in his honor, the Donald W. Cameron Campus. We also appreciate the cooperation and continuing efforts of the current president, Randy Parker, and members of the GTCC staff and community.

Our decision to showcase this particular college is not meant to imply that GTCC is the only community college worthy of serving as a model for others. We believe the examples speak for themselves, and we hope the book will bring valuable insight to current and aspiring college leaders. We look forward to continuing to learn and share the story of the nation's community colleges.

REFERENCES

Kinard, L. W., Jr. (2008). *Guilford Technical Community College, 1958–2008: Creating entrepreneurial partnerships for workforce preparedness.* Durham, NC: Carolina Academic Press.

INTRODUCTION

John E. Roueche and Suanne D. Roueche

The challenges that community colleges face today are not new ones. For many years, colleges have seen a shortfall in funding even as the demand for services increases. Community colleges face competition for resources and for students, and keeping up with the pace of technology requires constant attention. Although the challenges are many and multifaceted, they all originate with one central challenge: Doing more with less. The dichotomy that exists between funding decline and enrollment growth has only become more pronounced because of two realities:

- Local, state, and federal funding levels are unlikely to return to or even get close to their previous levels of 20–30 years ago, any time in the foreseeable future, if ever, for the large majority of education institutions.
- Enrollments are likely to continue to climb, fueled by the growing number of students who now more than ever need access to affordable higher education and support services.

This introduction examines what these realities mean for colleges in general and summarizes some of the key strategies colleges are implementing to cope with the funding decline–enrollment growth dichotomy. There are two arenas for which lack of funding has significant implications for ensuring student success while also ensuring institutional accountability: programs and services, and technology.

THE IMPLICATIONS OF DOING MORE WITH LESS

Finding New Ways to Provide Programs and Services

Because colleges must embrace, support, and serve the students they have, not the students they used to have, wish they had, or perhaps could have in the future, they must ramp up programs to embrace a diverse range of student needs, skill levels, and interests. Some students arrive academically underprepared for college-level work; others are college-ready but seek the course work that will enable them to transfer to a 4-year institution. For those seeking direct entry into the workforce, training needs range from the basic to the sophisticated, depending on the career goal. Their ages range from young adult to mature adult. They may come from dire economic circumstances that require hours of work outside school and the home, from positions of responsibility for providing family support, and from countries abroad. They all represent monumental challenges for recruitment and retention. Keeping the doors open for all of these students requires

- Having programs available to take them as they are, at their current academic levels, and preparing them adequately for either future academic or career opportunities.
- Reaching down into high schools to help prepare future and dual-credit students.
- Approaching workplaces to offer news about training and retraining, to encourage new development, and to provide opportunities for the recently unemployed.
- Serving students whose nontraditional needs (e.g., for flexible scheduling, lower tuition, etc.) are not being met by traditional institutions.

The implication of funding declines on the community college's ability to address this wide range of needs is clear: Availability of funding drives decisions about which programs will stay and which will go, it shapes directives for new programs, and it necessitates assessing the cost-effectiveness of all efforts. Management expert Peter Drucker said, "an enterprise that has sailed in calm waters for a long time ... needs to cleanse itself of the products, services, ventures that only absorb resources; the products, services, ventures that have become 'yesterday'" (2002, p. 43). For community colleges to stay current, they need to find new ways of doing business.

Keeping Current With Technology

If there were ever a time for colleges to be technologically savvy, it is now. The current student success and completion agenda requires that colleges have the means to collect, analyze, and communicate a wide range of performance data. Technology is equally critical for developing and delivering programs and courses in innovative and effective ways that promote academic success for students. Other benefits for students may include a streamlined and more accessible enrollment process, as well as online courses and student services. At the institutional level, the ability to collect and maintain data is critical to every aspect of institutional performance. The existence of reliable data informs decisions about programs and services and allows the institution to articulate how its student success goals are being met, both of which are also critical to attracting new capital for future growth.

The technology challenge is particularly daunting in light of decreased funding. Colleges must perform a balancing act to invest in technology that simultaneously supports the students and the institution. When funding is limited, colleges often have to make hard choices: Hiring an IT professional to meet the college's technology needs may mean cutting a program or service or not hiring the new faculty it needs.

RIDING OUT THE STORM

A chilling observation posed by a report from the Educational Testing Service (ETS; 2007), *America's Perfect Storm: Three Forces Changing Our Nation's Future,* captures the essence of the challenges resulting from the dichotomy of funding decline and enrollment growth. The report describes three forces as follows:

- Large numbers of people do not have the skills needed to be effective in an increasingly competitive workplace. Furthermore, skills are not evenly distributed across groups defined by race/ethnicity, origin, and socioeconomic status.
- Significant change in the U.S. economy has resulted in technological change and globalization, for which higher-level skills are required. For those who do not acquire competitive skills, the "economic future can be quite dismal" (ETS, 2007, p. 6).
- Demographic trends portend substantial increases in racial/ethnic diversity of the population over the next 20–25 years and beyond.

The report continues on the theme that the education and skill levels of all U.S. residents must be raised, but how human capital is distributed is just as important to the economy and our society as the growth of human capital:

> America's perfect storm is greater than the simple sum of the three sets of forces. . . The confluence of those forces can create a powerful dynamic that continually feeds the storm—putting at risk not only greater numbers of individuals but the very fabric of our nation. A future reflecting the projected changes in demographics and skill distributions is one in which there would be fundamental changes in existing economic and social structures. The implicit promise of every individual having a fighting chance to improve his or her station in life would be replaced by the reality of what columnist David Brooks has called an "inherited meritocracy." (ETS, 2007, pp. 24–25)

STRATEGIES FOR STRETCHING THE DOLLARS

Forging Strategic Alliances

To help them weather the economic downturn and expend their resources on securing their best efforts and programs the foreseeable future, many colleges form alliances with other colleges, business and industry, communities, the state, and government agencies. Such alliances are a trademark of innovative colleges and have many potential benefits in addition to cost savings. They can support community and workforce development; open up opportunities for partnerships with other academic institutions, industry, and international partners; increase fundraising opportunities; and raise the college's visibility in the community.

Successful colleges are willing to constantly assess and reassess alliances to determine which ones promise to be the most productive and beneficial in the long term and which ones may no longer be worth maintaining. They must identify and establish relationships that they really want, provide the impetus and the motivation for others to join them in establishing those relationships, recognize those that they are capable of establishing, and establish only those that they are willing to sustain over the long haul or at least for the foreseeable and viable future. There are few places left where going it alone in today's economic environment can be sustained. Establishing strong partnerships—especially friend raising (not just fundraising)—within the community, even long before critical needs are recognized, helps create a strong foundation for future support of programs and services that benefit community constituencies directly. Successful colleges find it good planning to be in the company of friends and supporters in any circumstances.

Linking to the Community

Setting realistic goals for meeting the community's needs is an important responsibility for a community college. To meet its workforce development goals, the college must consider doing those things that are best for the community, even if there appears to be no direct benefit the college. Establishing a middle college that helps students earn their high school degrees may seem beyond the mission of a community college, but in fact both the college and community will benefit if those students earn their degrees, continue seamlessly into college courses, and earn skills and credentials that help them enter the workforce.

Many colleges with an entrepreneurial spirit seek the advantages often associated with becoming a nexus, or hub, for community leadership. They participate in an established network of institutions, businesses, community agencies, and funding entities, from high schools to volunteer agencies and the courts, or help establish a new network of partners and supporters specific to an initiative or need. They seek being seen and serving as catalysts for community development, stepping up to address the problems of the community and tying responses from diverse entities together. In general, they look to being a constant resource for action, determining the fiscal, logistical, and support parameters for meeting the community's needs. Although economic and workforce development initiatives are hand-in-glove commitments to community, colleges often must make critical choices about the appropriate balance required to avoid overburdening programs and faculty and to maintain college services at necessary levels.

Community colleges should not have to choose between being institutions of higher learning and providers of services for community development. This is where strategic alliances come in. Partnerships are integral to a college's ability to address community problems that require long-term, systematic interventions. For example,

- Increasing student success in K–16 (kindergarten through college) schools across the city and county.
- Engaging citizens in forums to discuss community issues that affect the economic future.
- Presenting the community's best sides to businesses and industries considering a move to the area or establishing a new job-rich initiative.
- Providing opportunities for student internships in initiatives, programs, and organizations that can reinforce the concept of community service in the undergraduate experience.

Investing in People

First and foremost, community colleges are invested in the development of students, who are at the heart of the enterprise. It is for them that business must continue. However, colleges must invest equally in the faculty whose work it is to provide services that help students learn and, ultimately, be successful in achieving their academic and training goals. Colleges that pay special attention to attracting and retaining the best faculty make extraordinarily prudent, focused contributions to student success. These colleges engage faculty in opportunities to have their voices heard about issues that most affect the college, instruction, and professional growth and development, and then encourage faculty to be leaders at every level of the college. Investing in people extends outside the college as well, to those with whom the college forms partnerships, alliances, and other collaborations to support community and workforce needs. These people include the employers who help colleges identify the education needs of the unemployed and underemployed, as well as potential new workforce populations.

Fostering Institution-Wide Commitment

Transforming a college begins with the decision—individual and collective—to be committed to open doors, academic and program excellence, and making things happen. When a college is considering changes to its mission, to the ways it is organized, and to traditions that have been grounded in time and have become cultural habits of the organization, then it is setting about to become something different on a daily basis. Having made such a commitment also requires that change be scheduled, monitored, and evaluated.

As colleges discover that they must be more entrepreneurial, especially by relying less on state support and extramural funding, and becoming more strategic with, for example, their alliances, they may realize that there is more required to survive than even the most creative responses to its challenges to date. They must focus on ensuring that a can-do spirit permeates the institution and embrace the notion that the thinking of people within the institution will affect how well that spirit will drive appropriate, valuable change.

In *Guts! Companies That Blow the Doors Off Business-as-Usual*, Freiberg and Freiberg (2004) observed: "Heroes are ordinary people who make the routine extraordinary, regardless of their job descriptions or where they sit on the organizational chart. People who bring the best of who they are to work every day inspire others to do the same" (p. 218). Institutions do not change on their own; only the people in them can change themselves and effect change elsewhere, and these people must agree to believe in changing the ways in which they conduct the business of the institution. They must agree that student success is everyone's business, that recruitment and retention are everyone's responsibility. They look at the college from the perspective of the community, ask the question "what do you need and what have we done for you lately to meet those needs?" and attend to the answers. They embrace expanding technologies as ways to unite rather than alienate students, faculty, and staff. They embrace partnerships to keep their doors open. They understand that relationships built on trust, expertise, and commitment can be developed in-house among current faculty, staff, and administrators participating in leadership training. Such training establishes foundations upon which people can better themselves personally and improve their institutions professionally. And, their success in creating benchmark-quality programs and initiatives is further proof that the belief system works.

Addressing Institutional Effectiveness From Within

Many colleges that have looked to their communities for financial support and to business and industry for commendation and partnerships understand this reality: "… there isn't a business person … who makes a major investment and doesn't follow the dollar and look at performance" (Roser, 1996, A1). To remain relevant in their communities, colleges must provide clear indications of interest in improving their own performance relative to providing good service and turning out students who can perform on the job and in the next classroom.

Informed advisors (e.g., Ewell, 1993) suggest that colleges build the questions that external (and now many internal) stakeholders are asking into the next phases of their work, aligning their values with the values woven into public-policy conversations about effectiveness indicators. Unfortunately, more often than not, colleges are driven to change by outside pressures rather than by an internal charge to improve their own performance. External constituents are driven to ask why college leaders do not "initiate assessment so they can bring better arguments to the table" (Edgerton, 1990, p. 5).

Every state has accountability mandates, and because even more intrusive measures may be implemented with or without colleges' blessings, interest will continue to run high about student outcomes. Colleges will be expected to prove they can align expectations with realities. External calls for colleges to "explain themselves" continue to grow, and they come from entities that can effect change whether or not the colleges embrace the kind of change suggested. Internal and external pressures sustain the urgency to achieve greater transparency in all things affecting student performance and affected by student success. Colleges need to anticipate the potential for erosion of trust in higher education's ability to improve student performance, retention, and graduation, and meet that public perception with significant and positive change that sets improvement and better outcomes in motion.

Initiatives such as the Community College Survey of Student Engagement (CCSSE) and Achieving the Dream: Community Colleges Count (ATD) are successfully at work, just in time, at the right time, and for the right reasons. Both initiatives continue to test the college waters to determine whether and how well external initiatives can effect successful internal change in current practices and policies.

ATD is a long-term national initiative to help more community college students succeed—particularly those students who traditionally face the most significant barriers to success, including students of color, low-income students, and first-generation college students. The initiative is built on the belief that broad institutional change, informed by student achievement data, is critical to significantly improving student success rates (www.achievingthedream.org; McClenney & Mathis, 2011). Colleges join as members of ATD; each college is provided an ATD Coach to support the college's change initiatives.

The CCSSE, a product and service of the Center for Community College Student Engagement (CCCSE), is an established tool that helps institutions focus on good educational practice and identify areas in which they can improve their programs and services for students. Administered during the spring mostly to returning students, the CCSSE asks about institutional practices and student behaviors that are highly correlated with student learning and retention. The CCSSE serves as a complementary piece to the Survey of Entering Student Engagement (SENSE), with a more broad focus on the student experience. The center is housed at The University of Texas at Austin and is a membership-based initiative.

———————◆———————

From the bumpy financial experiences of the last 20+ years, we have learned that colleges will continue to be required to bounce back quickly from adverse situations. No one could predict with great accuracy or adequately describe the full measure of the impact that increasing enrollments and decreasing funding at all levels would have on all colleges in this last decade—especially on community colleges, which serve more than half of all undergraduates. Every challenge that one might document could be addressed in some positive way by an infusion of funds, but that is only half of the story.

There is much to be said for the creative adventures that can grow out of need and drive new thinking and resolve. If necessity is the mother of invention, and inspiration is driven by necessity, then community colleges may find that limited funds present one of their best opportunities to take to creative flight into new territories.

REFERENCES

Drucker, P. (2002). *Managing in turbulent times*. New York: HarperCollins.

Edgerton, R. (1990, September/October). Assessment at half-time. *Change, 22*, 4–5.

Educational Testing Service. (2007, January). *America's perfect storm: Three forces changing our nation's future*. Princeton, NJ: Author.

Ewell, P. T . (1993). The role of states and accreditors in assessment. In T. W. Banta & Associates (Eds.), *Making a difference: Outcomes of a decade of assessment in higher education.* San Francisco, CA: Jossey-Bass.

Freiberg, K., & Freiberg, J. (2004). *Guts! Companies that blow the doors off business-as-usual.* New York, NY: Doubleday.

McClenney, B., & Mathis, M. (2011). *Making good on the promise of the open door.* Washington, DC: Association of Community College Trustees.

Roser, M. A. (1996, November 10). Tenure faces biggest test as debate spills beyond academe. *Austin American-Statesman*, A1, A19.

SUGGESTED READING

Kanter, R. M. (1994, July/August). Collaborative advantage: The art of alliances. *Harvard Business Review, 72*(4), 96–108.

Roueche, J. E., Johnson, L. F., Roueche, S. D., & Associates. (1997). *Embracing the tiger: The effectiveness debate and the community college*. Washington, DC: Community College Press.

Roueche, J. E., & Jones, B. R. (2005). *The entrepreneurial community college.* Washington, DC: Community College Press.

Roueche, J. E., Richardson, M. M., Neal, P. W., & Roueche, S. D. (2008). *The creative community college: Leading change through innovation.* Washington, DC: Community College Press.

Roueche, J. E., Roueche, S. D., & Johnson, R. A. (2002, April/May). At our best: Facing the challenges of today and tomorrow. *Community College Journal*.

CHAPTER 1

Transformational Leadership: The Key to Meeting All Challenges

John E. Roueche and Suanne D. Roueche

The Challenge:
Providing the kind of leadership that can motivate a college to embrace new directions and practices to better serve its community.

The Response:
Communicating and sharing vision, persisting, cultivating problem seekers and solvers, listening, enabling and empowering others to lead, maintaining humor and humility, and recognizing the contributions of others.

The most successful leader of all is one who sees another picture not yet actualized. He sees the things which belong in the present picture but which are not yet there ... Above all, he should make his co-workers see that it is not his purpose which is to be achieved, but a common purpose born of the desires and the activities of the group.

—Mary Parker Follett (1941)

One cannot study the success of a college without looking carefully at the person at its helm. Guilford Technical Community College (GTCC) benefited from the consistent leadership of one president for two decades, and we highlight Donald Cameron's presidency in part because of this unusually long tenure, starting with his interim presidency in 1990 and installation as president in 1991 until his retirement in 2011. We observed and interviewed Cameron, and we interviewed internal and external stakeholders, including faculty and administrative staff, business and industry partners, and supporters. The portrait that emerged was one of a transformational leader who changed the culture and the face of an institution.

Like many community colleges, GTCC started small and grew, but it has always focused on preparing students to enter the technical workforce. In 1958 it began as the Guilford Industrial Education Center. In 1965 it began offering associate degrees and was renamed the Guilford Technical Institute. In 1983 it became Guilford Technical Community College with the addition of a college-transfer program. The third-largest community college in the state, GTCC has three campuses at Jamestown, High Point, and Greensboro, and it operates the T. H. Davis Aviation Center at Piedmont Triad International Airport (PTIA) and the Small Business Center in Greensboro (http://www.gtcc.edu). The aviation and transportation industries are central to the local economy.

As president, Cameron became known for forging strong partnerships with local industry and with the academic community, including the P–16 pipeline. Cameron took risks for a community college, such as starting a middle college (where high school students at risk of not graduating can earn both high school and college-level credit), a tech prep program (focusing on partnerships with industry), and the Larry Gatlin School of Entertainment Technology, with the collaboration of music star Larry Gatlin. In 2001 Cameron received the first President of the Year Award from the North Carolina State Board of Community Colleges, one of several recognitions he would receive for his contributions to the community. Subsequent chapters will explore some of GTCC's initiatives. In this chapter, we discuss leadership traits we believe are essential in a community college president, and we share insights from Gardner (1990) and other leadership strategists as well as observations from Cameron's presidency.

TRANSFORMATIONAL LEADERSHIP IN ACTION

Strong leaders are self-actualizing people known for setting high goals and achieving them, as people who exude the confidence to make things happen. Having the vision and being able to articulate that vision to others can change the dynamics from passive to active, from standing on the sidelines to being in the game. Knowledge of self is a key ingredient of effective leadership, that is, knowing one's strengths and how they fit with the organization's needs (see Bennis & Nanus, 1985).

In 2001, a reporter for the *News & Record* wrote of GTCC's negotiation of a successful business partnership. The reporter described Cameron, a former baseball catcher, this way: "From his crouch behind home plate, he adjusted the outfielders, shifted the infield, called the pitches. He was the backstop, and he relished it" (cited in Kinard, 2008, p.341). Speaking of his effort to develop the tech prep and middle college programs at GTCC, Cameron said: "During the development stage of these programs, I often felt like the coach I used to be. Often I needed to inspire others, sometimes to believe in an idea that they had doubts about, sometimes to move beyond their skepticism to give something at try" (Cameron, 2008, p. 37).

Articulating the Vision

A compelling vision is a catalyst for engaging others in doing important work. A shared vision is based on shared values—especially the values associated with hope and belief systems, in what one strives for and wants the future to hold. Those shared values are powerful links to engaging individuals in meaningful work that they can and must do together to make the vision happen.

A leader's vision must be articulated well; it must excite others into seeing the vision clearly and seeing themselves involved in the action, leading to their shared commitment to making it happen. Skillfully fulfilling one's role as visionary and dreamer, and documenting success, earns the confidence of others. Followers and colleagues alike can embrace such confidence—"just as our courage is so often a reflection of another's courage, so our faith is often in someone else's faith" (Gardner, 1990, p. 199, referring to William James's perspective on the power of confidence). Cameron could see and articulate the broader picture, and he put people in the positions where they needed to be to make it happen.

Bonita Wellington, human resources manager of Honda Aircraft, which partners with GTCC, said Cameron "nurtured the partnership by displaying his dynamic leadership style. He gets people's input, pulls resources together, and sets an example with his culture of responsiveness. He is simply a community asset … He gets the job done and doesn't miss a beat" (personal communication, August 17, 2010). Cameron earned a reputation for having "Guilford County's 'back' as GTCC's number one economic development player, coach, and general manager" (Kinard, 2008, p. 342).

Persistence of Vision

Gardner (1990) observed that "leaders, whose task it is to keep a society functioning, are always seeking the *common ground* that will make concerted action possible. They have no choice. It is virtually impossible to exercise leadership if shared values have disintegrated." Cameron sought common ground in 1999, when the local public school district, Guilford County Schools (GCS), selected a new superintendent, Terry Grier, who would come on board in 2000. Determined to ensure the continued success of GTCC's existing tech prep partnership with the district, Cameron scheduled a visit before Grier even arrived in North Carolina. He described the visit as follows:

> I journeyed to Franklin County, Tennessee, armed with evidence about our initiative. We met, and, frankly, it was an easy sell. Then he turned the tables and took me to Nashville Technical Institute where he had helped develop a middle college. At the end of my visit, he asked me to support the development of a middle college on GTCC's campus. I presented the concept at the next board meeting after my return to North Carolina. (Cameron, 2008, p. 34)

After many formal meetings and informal discussions, the public school board and the GTCC board decided to establish North Carolina's first middle college on the Jamestown Campus. A middle college allows an alternative path for local high school students who for varying reasons are underperforming in high school and are at risk of not graduating. The middle college draws them into another venue, the college campus, and provides an opportunity to take high school and college-level courses simultaneously in an effort to interest them in staying the course, graduating, and going on to college.

The middle college was a direct outcome of conversations between Grier and Cameron. Although Cameron's main interest was in maintaining and expanding GTCC's tech prep program, which he had initiated and developed with the school system, he was open to the request in return and became a strong advocate for the middle college concept. The middle college would reach out to students who otherwise might be lost to the educational system and become a financial burden on the community.

The tech prep program itself had been a difficult sell to the public schools early on; many of the high school principals did not see GTCC as "college of choice" for their students, but rather preferred them to move on to a "real college" elsewhere.

This issue was one that Cameron addressed and won when the partnerships were established to encourage high school students to take courses leading to GTCC's tech prep initiatives and courses. With the middle college idea, Cameron knew he would be going back to sell his own board and his faculty and staff to take on a new role and accept a new cohort of students that would test their mettle and break new ground on a college campus. He prevailed, along with the new superintendent, in selling it to the public schools and the college.

As of 2008, GTCC's middle colleges had a graduation rate of 85%, compared with a 63% rate for the county's traditional high schools. The GTCC middle colleges have received awards for outstanding performance, and students and graduates have been featured in local and state newspaper stories, in *Newsweek*, and on the CBS Evening News for their success in continuing academics and in the workplace (Cameron, 2008). Cameron observed that the students' stories were "even more remarkable considering that almost all of the students enrolled in the middle college were either high school dropouts at the time or had been identified as students likely to drop out" (p. 36).

Visitors from institutions across the state come to see the program as they pursue developing similar programs of their own. The relationship with GCS is strengthened, and the middle college faculty engage in joint professional development opportunities with the GTCC faculty and staff. Overall, the middle college has become a successful recruiting tool for the college, with 86% of the GTCC Middle College graduates continuing their education at GTCC (Cameron, 2008). (*See* also chapter 4.)

Cameron (2008) pointed out that "programs ... do not happen because of one player; that would be impossible. The superintendent and I had to be team players for Tech Prep and the middle college, and we had to ensure that our staff members were team players as well" (p. 37). "Dozens of logistical details had to be worked out: All ... were solved, in large part, because the new superintendent and I worked closely together on the implementation" (p. 35). Cameron noted that the trip to Tennessee to meet the new superintendent in advance "was pivotal to our future work" (p. 37).

Leaders who have demonstrated great patience and resolve "have learned that the system will respond if they work at it long enough and hard enough; and if this fails to work, they have ideas about rejuvenating the system" (Burns & Sorenson, 1999, p. 300). Cameron wrote, "This is a story of slow and profound change. The changes [developing mutually beneficial relationships between a public school system and a community college] took 25 years" (Cameron, 2008, p. 37).

Similarly, Cameron championed the North Carolina Center for Global Logistics, where potential students can inquire about how best to proceed with their searches for specific training venues. The center requires the partnership of all higher education entities in the region. It is a consumer advocacy effort with the goal of providing the best information relative to training programs, without regard for whether a particular institution would benefit directly. Foundation board member Jim Morgan noted:

Cameron went to every higher education leader in the region and brought all of them on board except one. Now, people can call and ask where they should take a particular course. He made them want to be a part of something because he showed them how special it was. It is not easy to bring people together when they're in competition with one another. He made this idea happen, and now it is here." (personal communication, August 18, 2010)

The center provides a state-of-the-art clearinghouse for inquiries, education, outreach, and research through a collaborative public/private partnership among regional educational institutions. In addition, the initiative has been strengthened by the participation of businesses and industries in the 12-county Piedmont Triad Region. Having training resources and industry expertise in one location supports the logistics and distribution infrastructure and assists with marketing and recruitment.

Collective enthusiasm will carry the day through the usual cycles of hopefulness and hopelessness, of elation and despair. The patience and persistence a leader brings to the enterprise, the ability to articulate the goals for success with clarity and passion, will go the critical long way toward engaging others. Motivating and inspiring others is the real trick to getting all on board; knowing how to get others engaged with full commitment requires consistent application of the leader's most critical skill. Leadership genius "lies in the manner in which leaders see and act on their own and their followers' values and motivations" (Burns, 1978, p. 19). Clarifying a perception of that future helps successful leaders harness the power of individuals working together toward achieving common goals and nurtures the human relationships to bring compelling visions to life of what is not yet visible. Thus, they are able to draw out the best in themselves and in others.

Cultivating Problem Seekers and Solvers

Life requires unrelenting effort, a willingness to try—and humans are well fitted for the effort. We are not only problem solvers but also problem seekers. If a suitable problem is not at hand, we invent one. Most games are invented problems. We are designed for the climb, not for taking our ease, either in the valley or at the summit (see Gardner, 1990, p. 195).

Strong leaders surround themselves with problem solvers. Many of the transformational leaders we have studied expressed a strong bias toward seeking advice from a group selected to gather around a problem and solve it, to bring their unique perspectives to the table. They were not shy about accepting the help and advice of others, nor were they shy about making a final decision, made even better by the balance brought about by focused problem-solving discussions,

Moreover, leaders are biased toward problem seekers. One would have to ask why anyone would encourage problem seeking when there are plenty of problems to go around. Having asked that, we learned that a strong bias toward being the best you can be drives the question: "Are we the best college we can be, and if not, what must we do to be that college?" If the answer is "yes," then the die is cast. A parallel to that answer was expressed by Gardner (1990): "When a golden age subsides, the genetic possibilities in the population have not changed. The human material remains. But the dream and the drama have ended" (p. 193). As Edmund Gleazer, president emeritus of the American Association of Community Colleges, asked: "How do you get the challenge back into the institution? How do you sharpen the cutting edge? (1998, p. 161).

There can also be significant advantages to giving others experiences outside their own institutions—for example, having faculty visit other institutions and observe successful practices and situations similar to their own. Leaders who encourage this are committed to avoiding the disadvantages of a too-narrow view of the world, aptly described by the dog sled musher who observed: "the view only changes for the lead dog." Problem seekers can be valuable contributors to mission accomplishment, because they may be able to identify problems that might go unnoticed by others with less well-trained eyes. They are astute in asking the questions about how the college can better serve its community, seeing things that others cannot see. And, oftentimes, it means becoming active participants in programs that may well be on the edge of one's mission. As Cameron (2008) wrote of two relatively high-risk efforts:

> For me, implementation of both the Tech Prep program and the middle college was clearly part of our college's mission. It is true that the middle college was more on the edge of our mission, but I knew it was important for the community. Sometimes we need to remind ourselves that an important aspect of the mission of a community college is to assist in solving community problems, even if there is no obvious and direct benefit to the college in doing so. (pp. 37–38)

When the GTCC middle college was gearing up, Cameron and Grier made a point to "speak from the same script." Cameron reported that within GTCC, he made the middle college one of his key initiatives, introducing the middle college faculty and staff at various meetings throughout the year, talking about its successes. "My plan was to make the middle college faculty feel like a part of the college community and to help GTCC's faculty and staff see the connections between our missions and work. I believe the plan was successful" (Cameron, 2008, p. 35).

Choosing the right personnel was essential to winning over critics on both sides of the table. The superintendent chose an excellent candidate for the founding principal and other positions on the middle college staff, "professionals with proven records and faculty and staff who had strong reputations for being student focused" (Cameron, 2008, p. 35). Cameron also noted that the success of the middle colleges could be attributed in part to the selection of a respected GTCC faculty member, Jane Pendry, as the first college liaison. She was instrumental in working out details of the middle college and persuading critics away from potentially negative viewpoints about allowing younger students, already somewhat disenfranchised, to come on campus and participate academically.

The Art of Listening

Active, sincere, focused listening with purpose evokes respect. Active listeners indicate their respect for the ideas, feelings, thoughts, and comments of others by giving them the gifts of time and energy attending to what they are hearing. Foundation board member Jim Morgan said of Cameron: "His listening skills are key; he comes up with a win-all situation … Cameron welcomes change with his unique listening skills … he keeps good employees. When I talk about good employees, I mean that he wants their input. He wants people smarter than he is around so they can learn from each other" (personal communication, August 18, 2010).

In a study of 10 colleges recognized as having high staff morale, Rice and Austin (2001) learned that willingness to share information was one of the key discriminating characteristics: "The sharing of information—and the sense of trust that permeates these institutions—fosters … respect" (p. 51). Wilhelmina Delco, who served for 20 years with the Texas House of Representatives and was a founding member of the Austin Community College Board of Trustees, warned future college leaders: "What people don't understand, they vote against" (University of Texas, 2010). Keeping others in the appropriate loops, being open to questions, and responding consistently and accurately are imperative to keeping people on board and, if not totally positive, then perhaps keeping them neutral. In 2010, GTCC director of eLearning, Brenda Kays, wrote that Cameron "instills 'consistency of message' and examines data. It is the same message delivered consistently to all stakeholders" (personal communication, August 17, 2010).

Enabling and Empowering Others to Lead

Leaders provide the links among individuals to improve communication and encourage discussion, which facilitates consensus (Burns, 1978, p. 20). We believe that the most successful leaders do this as a silent partner. As interpreted by Stephen Mitchell (1988), the Chinese philosopher Lao Tzu observed of leaders:

> A leader is best when people barely know that he exists, not so good when people obey and acclaim him, worst when they despise him. "Fail to honor people, and they fail to honor you." But of a good leader, who talks little, when his work is done, his aim fulfilled, they will all say, "We did this ourselves." (Laozi & Mitchell, 1988, p. 20)

Helping others build confidence in themselves is an important task for a leader and is especially difficult in challenging economic times when positive thinking is essential to maintaining motivation to make progress despite the challenges. The focus must be on living up to one's or an institution's potential. James MacGregor Burns said of Woodrow Wilson that he had the unique ability to lift an entire nation of people "out of their everyday selves … and *into* their better selves" (1978, p. 462).

Strong leaders see the potential and talent in others, including those who may not recognize it in themselves, and they publicly identify and recognize it. The response by the recipient to such recognition is often a catalyst for extraordinary effort. As Gardner (1990) stated, "In the conventional mode people want to know whether the followers believe in the leaders; a more searching question is whether the leader believes in the followers" (p. 199).

Strong and effective leaders characteristically demonstrate trust in others to make good decisions and develop strategies to implement them. In colleges focusing on leadership development, to encourage and support and train leaders at all levels of the institution, participants find that they are brought into compelling discussions about issues and challenges, problems and responses, collaborative strategies, and relationship-building activities among individuals who are working in and across small and large college settings. Across the board, establishing unique initiatives for the purpose of "investing in their own" are win–win opportunities to help keep everyone pulling in the same direction, on common ground, toward shared goals.

Cameron wrote about the entrepreneurial, risk-taking activities that characterized many of the projects that GTCC sought out and embraced. Many, he observed, would not have been possible "if those involved had limited their thinking to the boundaries of existing financial resources available to the college" and had not been willing to take on "a certain amount of risk," including the risk that even "successfully initiated projects [might not] live up to their long-term promise" (Cameron, 2005, pp. 60–61).

The eLearning program was such a challenge for GTCC early on. Although Cameron and others agreed the eLearning program was necessary—providing students with 24/7 access—the program had to be implemented correctly to win over faculty and administrators who understandably suspected it could be just one more initiative to strain an already tight budget. That "winning over" required that everyone recognize eLearning as a "student-centered" program that appeals to students who do not necessarily engage in the face-to-face group atmosphere of instruction.

Director Kays observed, "some students feel safer in the online environment," (personal communication, August 17, 2010), especially the most recent generations of students who enjoy personal communication online via social networking sites. But the challenges of operating the eLearning program included convincing executive leadership of the need for attention to critical details, including availability of faculty for the program and funds for other resources needed to ensure program effectiveness. There were the additional challenges of creating and implementing a faculty-created course evaluation tool (a 2-year process), and requiring faculty to be certified to teach in the program, especially learning to create online classrooms that are dynamic, active places for learning and keeping students in the loop to avoid their feeling isolated in their studies.

To help ease the transition from classroom to online classroom, faculty were required to train for the assignments by taking training online themselves and learning well how students face working online. The eLearning program continued to be a work in progress, with the president's trust and support. Kays remarked: "Cameron steps back to enable me to run with my passion for the eLearning program." (personal communication, August 18, 2010).

Employing Humor and Humility

Gardner (1990) observed that we spend most of our lives thinking about the impact and the influence others have had on our lives and that it is only when we have reached a significant level of maturity that we begin to realize the impact we have had on the lives of others. That impact cuts both ways, as sharing expressions of despair, negativity, and hopelessness are as contagious as are expressions of joy, positivity, and hope. Being a cheerleader for the college and demonstrating credible behavior means keeping a positive public face and not getting bogged down in the pathology of a bad moment in order to keep morale high and others engaged in the effort.

While humor may not be a statistically significant personality trait for outstanding leaders, we believe it is critical to working with others. Lee W. Kinard said Cameron would "exercise guilt and humor to get the job done" (2008, p. 342). When Cameron had the opportunity to work with music star Larry Gatlin to discuss the possibility of starting a country music school at the college, Cameron kept his sense of humor and his flexibility in pursuit of his dream:

> Cameron's idea of a "school of country music" piqued Gatlin's imagination, but the entertainer found the vision narrow and told him so with a curt "I don't like 'country music.'" But Gatlin remained positive: "Let's call it the Larry Gatlin School of Entertainment!" Cameron acquiesced, "Larry, if we can use your name, we will call it anything you want" (Kinard, 2008, p. 324).

Recognizing the Contributions of Others

Strong leaders understand the importance of recognizing the efforts of others, rewarding the hard work of the larger group or community. Not only do they identify accomplishments and effort, they do it publicly, both at the college and on larger stages, locally, regionally, and nationally. Recognition strategies such as employee-of-the-month awards, scholarships to students in the name of meritorious faculty, and leadership development initiatives that fuel succession planning and encourage leadership at all levels showcase outstanding service to the institution and make positive statements about the primacy of the work of others.

In *The Entrepreneurial Community College,* Cameron (2005) wrote:

> Within the college community, I encouraged all campus employees to assume a role in collegewide planning processes. Through their participation, individual employees were able to demonstrate high regard

for initiative, creativity, and risk taking. The employee-of-the-month award was established to recognize creativity in performing the jobs more effectively, conserving college resources, and providing improved customer service. (p. 52)

When Cameron himself was recognized by the Joseph M. Bryan Foundation of Greater Greensboro, Inc., as the Unsung Hero for community service in 2005, Cameron said, "there's only one way you can become an unsung hero and that's by having 300 to 400 people working with you who are committed to changing the community by helping citizens grow their lives and careers" (cited in Kinard, 2008, p. 390).

OBSERVATIONS FROM BOARD MEMBERS AND INDUSTRY LEADERS

The lessons we learned from Cameron's leadership were informed by three people who watched Cameron and the college in action over a significant period of time: Stuart B. Fountain, who served as a member of the GTCC Board of Trustees for 20 years, and as chair of the presidential selection committee that named Cameron in 1991; J. Patrick Danahy, member of the GTCC Board of Trustees since 1994, and founding president of the Greensboro Partnership in 2006 (a CEO consortium dedicated to economic development); and Scott Ralls, president, North Carolina Community College. Following is a summary of their comments offered during Cameron's presidency.

- This president surrounds himself with strong, smart, competent people, some whom others might find threatening. He says that he wants individuals around him that are "smarter than himself," have reputations for being plainspoken and often opinionated, with good reason to be so. He wants to be around the people who are best for the roles they are hired to play. He listens to them; they inform his decisions; he brings broad thinkers to the table. He is not egocentric.
- This president is a risk-taker—The Larry Gatlin School of Entertainment idea was an uncanny risk. The president is a good, honest man, but the risk-taking element and his insight into people and needs of his community are added bonuses, real plusses for this college.
- This president sees into the future—10 to 15 years down the road—and how the various pieces will fit together and where the resources to support the puzzle fitting together will come from and how they will be sustained. His insight about a Northwest campus, way out in the country, was strategic. The North Carolina Center for Global Logistics needed a home, and Cameron saw it not only as a hub for collaborative efforts and initiatives but as a strong nexus that would further support what appeared, at first, to be a remote spot for another GTCC campus. The alignment worked, and the Northwest campus became reality.

- This president is a person of the community; he has been on every board it has—foundations, chambers of commerce, bond campaigns. And with that, he is exceptional at putting different pieces of our community together to get an excellent product. He does it in a way that makes everyone feel good about the roles they will play, and in the final product. He sits at the table, but he doesn't look for credit.
- This president does not ask others to do anything he would not do himself.
- This president adopted the position that he worked for others; he is a servant leader, in its best and simplest sense, not sitting on top of everyone and everything, but serving alongside others who are working toward the same goals.
- This president is the best salesman (for the community and the state) we have.
- This president is right most of the time, and that doesn't hurt!
- This president doesn't change; he is the same person today that he was yesterday or last year or will be in the future. What he says you can take to the bank or take to heart. His vision and his values don't change.
- This president has made GTCC a manufacturing facility that produces graduates; he focuses on students, on what will make them successful, finding out what makes them successful. These efforts make our engine more efficient. Student success drives the college train, fuels its engine. Developmental education initiatives, Achieving the Dream outcomes, and the Gates Foundation support are hallmarks of improved student performance and consistent reminders of GTCC's reason to be.
- This president has made GTCC a "training ground" for innovative leaders. He has created a culture that pays attention to giving others room to grow.

LESSONS LEARNED

From these insights, leaders might consider the following lessons:

- Leaders should surround themselves with smart people who are honest, competent, and unafraid to voice their opinions.
- Leaders should listen to the people they have chosen to be on the team.
- Leaders should always look to the future and have a plan.
- Leaders should be visible in the community.
- Leaders should be reliable advocates and friends to the community.
- Leaders should be servant leaders.
- Leaders should be consistent and trustworthy in attitude, communications, and business practices.

REFERENCES

Bennis, W. G., & Nanus, B. (1985). *Leaders: The strategies for taking charge*. New York, NY: HarperBusiness.

Burns, J. M. (1978). *Leadership*. New York, NY: Harper & Row.

Burns, J. M., & Sorenson, G. J. (1999). *Dead center: Clinton-Gore leadership and the perils of moderation*. New York, NY: A Lisa Drew Book, Simon & Schuster, Inc.

Cameron, D. W. (2005). Entrepreneurial partnerships. In J. E. Roueche & B. R. Jones, *The entrepreneurial community college* (pp. 51–61). Washington, DC: Community College Press.

Cameron, D. W. (2008). Guilford Technical and Community College: A story of patience, persistence, perception, and change. In J. E. Roueche, M. M. Richardson, P. W. Neal, & S. D. Roueche, *The creative community college: Leading change through innovation* (pp. 27–38). Washington, DC: Community College Press.

Follett, M. P. (1941). *Dynamic administration*. New York: Harper.

Gardner. J. W. (1990). *On leadership*. New York, NY: The Free Press.

Gleazer, E. J., Jr. (1998). (1980). *The community college: Values, vision and vitality*. Washington DC: American Association of Community Colleges.

Kinard, L. W., Jr. (2008). *Guilford Technical Community College, 1958–2008: Creating entrepreneurial partnerships for workforce preparedness*. Durham, NC: Carolina Academic Press.

Laozi, & Mitchell, S. (1988). *Tao te ching: A new English version*. New York: Harper & Row.

Miller, A. D. (2010, August 24). Opinion. *Austin American-Statesman*.

Rice, R. E., & Austin, A. E. (2001). High faculty morale: What exemplary colleges do right. In J. E. Roueche, E. E. Ely, & S. D. Roueche, *In pursuit of excellence* (pp. 51–58). Washington, DC: Community College Press.

The University of Texas at Austin. (2010, November 8). Presentation at the meeting of the Community College Leadership Program, Austin, TX.

SUGGESTED READING

Gardner, D., & Barnett, E. (2003, Spring). Learning colleges and educational change: An interview with Terry O'Banion. *Update: On research and leadership, 14*(2). Champaign, IL: University of Illinois. Retrieved from http://occrl.ed.uiuc.edu/Newsletter/2203/spring/spring2003_1.asp

Roueche, J. E., Baker III, G. A., & Rose, R. R. (1989). *Shared vision: Transformational leadership in American community colleges*. Washington, DC: Community College Press.

Roueche, J. E., & Roueche, S. D. (2007). The art of visionary leadership: Painting a face on the future. *Celebrations*. Austin, TX: The University of Texas at Austin, National Institute for Student and Institutional Development.

CHAPTER 2

Preparing for Leadership Succession

Martha M. Ellis

The Challenge:
Ensuring that professionals throughout the college are prepared to assume greater responsibility to fill vacant leadership positions seamlessly.

The Response:
Keeping the leadership pipeline full by putting leadership development pathways and opportunities in place.

In keeping with the GTCC mission to provide access to lifelong learning opportunities for personal growth, workforce productivity, and community service, I commit my passion and enthusiasm to help people enhance their development and use their talents in their chosen careers so that they can live purposeful lives.

—Donald Cameron (2010, p. 1)

No doubt, there are days when—as a president, vice president, dean, or department chair—you wonder what will happen when you leave your college for a new position, retirement, or just a vacation. You wonder if the successful initiatives that have begun will continue and mature. What can you provide to the leadership team so they will be successful today and in the future? What is your plan for passing on the passion and leadership to others?

Community colleges are experiencing a leadership challenge as many current leaders and faculty members retire. Some national studies have projected a tidal wave of retirements (e.g., Weisman & Vaughan, 2007). Although we know this will happen, higher education as a whole is generally not doing significant work to prepare. Developing competent leaders is central to the future success of the mission of colleges as they address the social, economic, and technological forces that are forging an extraordinary period of change and a time of opportunity.

Colleges are complex organizations that create critical challenges for their leaders and require them to mobilize everyone at their colleges to work toward a shared vision. Current and future leadership gaps can be addressed through a variety of well-planned and coordinated opportunities that can help meet the needs that the gaps create. This type of leadership planning is the process of identifying key needs of the college for intellectual activities and leadership competencies across campuses over the upcoming years. Once the key needs are identified, then preparing colleagues from within the college for present and future responsibilities for the short- and the long-term begins. This approach is described as "growing your own" at all levels of the institution, so that the college mission and vision can be passed on from one generation to the next.

SUCCESSION PLANNING

Adopting a Succession Planning Framework

Community colleges and universities will soon experience a dearth of leadership due to impending retirements of department heads, deans, vice presidents, and presidents. Succession planning is the process of pinpointing key needs for intellectual talent and leadership throughout the organization over time and preparing colleagues for present and future work needed by the organization to maintain current positions and improve upon others as needed. The process focuses on developing employees for promotion within the organization (see Rothwell, 2010).

Recognizing this national trend, Guilford Technical Community College (GTCC) president Donald Cameron requested an assessment of all employees currently in leadership positions who met the eligibility guidelines for retirement under the North Carolina State Retirement plan (age 65, with 5 years credited service; age 60, with 25 years of credited service; or any age, with 30 years of credited service). Nearly 30% of GTCC's leaders, including Cameron himself, met the guidelines and requirements for retirement eligibility. Cameron knew that the future of GTCC depended on having qualified, well-trained leaders. He took action. In 2005, the office of Organizational Development was established, and a director was hired. The director is responsible for developing, directing, coordinating, and evaluating a comprehensive professional development program, which includes succession planning. A comprehensive notebook is provided to all employees and managers to assist in the implementation of the college's structured, formal, and informal leadership development program.

Succession planning at GTCC is a process of preparing the college for the future. Providing continuity for the college through changes in leadership is critical to the college, the students, and the community. The goal is to facilitate the development of leadership competencies and strategies in an effort to build a talented and diverse group of leaders who will leverage their human assets for the success of students and the college. The process of leadership development is one of transformation, whereby leaders are encouraged to experiment and to make the leap to gaining a deeper understanding of themselves, the college, the world, and their relationships to others. GTCC adopted a framework to provide the college with a process for ensuring institutional effectiveness as the college family develops and retains its most valuable asset—talented people. The framework is depicted in Figure 2.1.

Cascading Leadership Model

To assist in shifting the culture and practice at GTCC to one of access, student success, and data analysis in decision making and management, the college invested in training on designated Achieving the Dream (ATD) interventions for a cadre of employees. For example, more than 40 faculty and staff members were trained to teach

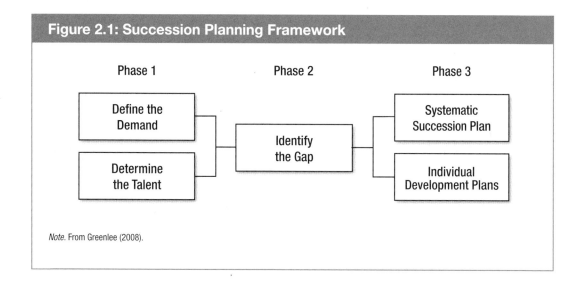

Figure 2.1: Succession Planning Framework

Phase 1   Phase 2   Phase 3

Define the Demand

Determine the Talent

Identify the Gap

Systematic Succession Plan

Individual Development Plans

Note. From Greenlee (2008).

a student success course. GTCC also applied the train-the-trainer model, devoting dollars and time to select faculty and staff so that these employees became on-site trainers later on.

To promote and secure an understanding of the data and provide skills for data analysis that could be applied to improved student success, GTCC developed a "cascading leadership" model. The philosophical underpinning of the model is that a change in employee behavior is best stimulated by action or intervention by the employee's direct supervisor in the leadership chain. For example, the executive team worked with division heads, who in turn worked with the department chairs in looking at and analyzing data. The next year, the department chairs worked with the faculty within their departments on data analysis.

Data analysis is appropriately conducted at the faculty level, so that faculty can then use the collected data to impact classroom and pedagogical practice to increase student success. Transmitting leadership from the institutional to the divisional to the departmental to the individual level brought about cultural change and embedded ATD goals into the college's daily processes. The dissemination of data analysis training is one example of cascading leadership in action. Empowering individual employees across the college to provide leadership and take calculated risks in their daily activities allows them to be more fulfilled professionally and to play a major role in helping achieve the college's mission.

GTCC'S GROWING YOUR OWN PHILOSOPHY

GTCC's leaders, including Cameron and the GTCC Board of Trustees, recognized that moving the college from "good to complete or great" required investing time and money in opportunities for employee development activities and experiences at all levels of the college. They recognized that growing and empowering their own leaders was an important investment for the future of the college. Employee leadership development has emerged as a foundation for achieving GTCC's vision and mission. Cultivating, nourishing, supporting the vision by weaving it into the cultural fabric of the college requires patience, perseverance, and commitment. The college's leadership team recognizes that human resources will give GTCC the all-important competitive edge to turn vision into reality and acknowledges that GTCC employees are the heart and soul of the college. Each day, these employees help students fulfill dreams, help industries grow the economy, and help local communities better provide for a robust quality of life.

By providing opportunities for growth and development, the college allows employees to improve and broaden their knowledge, skills, and abilities. This focus on continual improvement and change is critical to keeping the college moving forward. Supporting employees, students, and the community requires far more effort than mere skill development will provide. A systemic, integrated, continual process, rather than sporadic, disparate programs is GTCC's view of cascading leadership. Cascading leadership is built on the premise that employees throughout the institution can provide leadership.

For cascading leadership to be effective, employees must have the requisite knowledge and skills to make decisions and take calculated risks that are in line with the college's mission and vision. Employee development is a partnership between the college and each employee. The partnership requires time, energy, and commitment from each employee and from the college, and through this partnership, employees come to understand how they contribute to the big picture of the college's vision and mission. Employee development includes skill-specific learning, coupled with avenues for discourse and sharing of new ideas and processes. The needs of the individual, the institution, and the region are fused to form this partnership that promotes the potential of each employee through learning, discovery, problem solving, and involvement. According to GTCC's employee development philosophy,

- Employee development is a flexible process with growth options. The employees are the ultimate judge of their success and have the primary responsibility for individual development plans.
- Employee development is as diverse as are GTCC employees.
- Employee development spans the depth and breadth of experience, encompassing enhanced skills for the present job as well as preparation for broader or changing responsibilities.
- Employee development aligns individual goals with organizational needs.

The benefits of employee development for both the organization and the individual are described in Table 2.1.

GTCC's expectation is that leaders will develop GTCC's people (employees) and that employees will take responsibility for their own development while supporting the development of others around them. The college learned that, for this expectation to be successful, roles must be defined clearly to meet these expectations. Employees have the primary responsibility for their career development by assessing skills, values, and interests; developing individual plans; and utilizing the tools and opportunities provided to them. Managers are responsible for assessing employees' skills and capabilities and providing accurate and timely feedback on performance. Managers also assist employees in utilizing tools and formulating development plans. The college supports employee development by encouraging professional growth and providing necessary tools and opportunities. Employees compile development plans based on the following:

- Past performance, based on appraisals and feedback from managers.
- Current performance, based on requirements and expectations of their current position as well as performance standards and organizational goals.
- Future focus, based on talent assessment, individual career goals, and organizational strategic plans.

Employee development is integrated into solutions for addressing GTCC's challenges. The following sections present examples of employee development activities that GTCC has put in place for staff, faculty, and administrators.

Table 2.1: Benefits of Employee Development

Benefits for the College	Benefits for the Employee
- Contributes to achievement of organizational goals through skill development. - Strengthens leadership and technical skills. - Creates a highly talented workforce through continuous learning. - Builds depth of talent in the organization. - Prepares employees to meet the future needs of the college. - Supports retention of employees.	- Enables achievement of personal and career goals. - Establishes a link between organizational and personal goals. - Enhances current skills and performance. - Improves future performance. - Enhances employability. - Promotes purposeful lives.

TEACHING ASSOCIATE FACULTY-IN-TRAINING PROGRAM

With burgeoning student enrollments, community colleges often are challenged by having to identify and bring qualified adjunct instructors to the college. GTCC's Faculty-in-Training (FIT) program was established in 1999, in response to the college's need for hiring qualified adjunct instructors. Because the University of North Carolina–Greensboro (UNCG) cannot offer teaching assistantships to master's students, a partnership with GTCC was designed to benefit both institutions, by encouraging graduate students to explore a teaching career in community colleges. Associates gain teaching experience and understanding of community colleges in a mentored and supportive environment.

Teaching associate candidates must have at least 18 graduate hours in their teaching disciplines or have completed a master's degree and, in addition, have some teaching experience under their belts. Approximately 35 professionals apply each application period, and generally 15 move successfully through the application process. Upon acceptance, teaching associates receive a two-semester appointment, dependent upon receipt of a successful first-semester performance review. The associates are paid a stipend for the two semesters. Their responsibilities are as follows:

- Teach two courses each semester.
- Attend weekly seminars on topics such as learning styles, classroom management, distance learning, technology in the classroom, and cooperative learning.
- Prepare a videotaped lesson presentation to be critiqued by a mentor and other teaching associates.
- Observe the classrooms of full-time faculty teaching in the same field.
- Be observed in the classroom twice each semester.
- Serve the college 3 hours per week in areas such as the writing center, developing online curriculum, tutoring, serving on committees, and assisting with department needs.
- Complete a teaching portfolio that documents pedagogical skill development and basic knowledge of the community college philosophy.
- Work with a mentor.

Each teaching associate is assigned an experienced faculty member as a mentor. Mentors provide associates with opportunities to develop their own skills under the guidance of a skilled faculty member. Mentors are described as "half teacher, half cheerleader" (Buck & MacGregor, 2001). This supportive environment is critical to the success of the program. The FIT director is a faculty member with course-released time, the GTCC representative in the partnership with UNCG, and a point of contact for mentors. The director handles administrative functions for the program, coordinates the weekly seminars, and completes the final evaluation of each associate.

Eighty-six teaching associates completed the program between 1999 and 2010. Although the program began with graduate students who were interested in teaching English, the program has expanded to include associates interested in teaching many other disciplines, including history, political science, biology, nursing, advertising and graphic design, and information systems technology. Nine teaching associates have gone on to accept full-time positions with GTCC. Others have accepted positions at North Carolina A&T University, North Carolina State University, Wake Technical Community College, and Sandhills Community College. In addition, some associates have gone into PhD programs being offered at area universities.

In evaluations, associates have said that although the program can be overwhelming at times, the knowledge acquired is retained, and the supportive atmosphere promotes development of effective teaching skills. When asked to describe the benefits of the program, associates have cited the special relationships they form with each other in their cohort during the academic year. They share teaching strategies, classroom management skills, and support from positions of common experiences. Associates describe this camaraderie as beneficial in their exploration of a career in community college teaching and their development of a professional identity as a faculty member.

Leadership Effectiveness and Development Program

GTCC established the Leadership Effectiveness and Development Program (LEAD) to facilitate the development of leadership competencies and strategies to build talented and diverse groups of leaders who would play major roles in GTCC's future. The President's Leadership Seminar was its catalyst. The purpose of the annual seminar, first held in 1997, is to promote and strengthen GTCC's broad continuum of leadership potential to meet the challenges of the 21st century. The seminar is 4.5 days, made possible with funding from and sponsorship by the GTCC Foundation. Topics for the seminar include the mission and philosophy of the North Carolina Community College System, ethical leadership, and major issues and leadership in community colleges.

All regular full-time GTCC employees are invited to apply for approximately 20 slots that are open each year. Participants are selected based on demonstrated leadership potential, which includes participation in the work of college committees, projects, and organizations; participation in community activities; initiative in improving personal and career skills; and competence in handling assigned responsibilities. Participants are expected to attend all of the interactive learning workshops, take part in follow-up activities, and assume leadership roles in future GTCC projects and activities.

Upon successful completion of the President's Leadership Seminar, participants may elect to continue and build on this experience by engaging in a subsequent 10-month LEAD program. Eligible employees submit a letter of interest, along with a description of their leadership philosophy and a personal purpose statement. Participants form a cohort for whom mutual goals are aligned with major college initiatives while individual goals are tailored to meet the specific needs of each participant.

Since 1997, 197 employees have participated in the President's Leadership Seminar. Annual evaluations are held at the end of the seminar to determine program effectiveness and participants' gained knowledge. Two participants shared feedback about their experience:

> After participating in the President's Leadership Seminar, I am confident that I want to be a part of the team that will lead Guilford Technical Community College into the future. I believe that GTCC can provide me the avenue to achieve my aspirations if I provide the dedication and determination.

> I feel privileged to have been part of what has happened this week. I will work diligently to take all that I learned and put it into practice. The entire seminar was absolutely top notch.

To date, 48 employees who completed the President's Leadership Seminar have been promoted into positions of leadership at GTCC or other institutions. The GTCC positions fall along a wide range of responsibilities and service—including custodial manager, bursar, division chair, and vice president. In addition, participants completing the seminar have taken positions as vice presidents and presidents at other community colleges. Fifty-seven employees have graduated from the LEAD program from 2005 to 2010.

EMPLOYEE TRAINING: IMPROVING STUDENT SUCCESS BY BREAKING DOWN STAFF SILOS

Student evaluations informed GTCC that students' initial experience was confusing and frustrating. Students were receiving inconsistent information, having to navigate multiple offices, and dealing with inaccurate data entry. As is described in chapter 3, GTCC revamped the intake process through creation of a Front-Door Center and reorganization and training of personnel. Like many colleges, GTCC designed a one-stop shop for enrollment, with a single reception area for admissions, records, and financial aid—created with placement testing across the hall in one direction, counseling and disability services across the hall in another direction, and cashiers a few steps down the hall. Orientation, counseling, and mentoring groups for minority male students are facilitated out of this space, as well.

As with many colleges, silos developed in the enrollment process arena. To break down the silo effect that was characteristic of the various student services, employees were provided with cross-training and co-location. Training for staff members who interface with students and the public in person and by phone reduced the amount of conflicting information, provided as much as 80% of information needed in one visit or phone call, and improved student experiences. Customer-service training assisted with student interaction and conflict reduction during the enrollment process. Job shadowing became part of professional development experiences, enabling departments to understand workloads and challenges of each area. Assessment of employee personalities, as well as their skills, facilitated a good match for the employee and the goals of the new front-door initiative.

GTCC discovered that intensive employee cross-training activities were necessary prior to implementation of the one-stop shop. In addition, continuous weekly training was necessary to keep silos from reforming and to keep staff members up-to-date on information. The college is committed to providing dedicated time to ongoing training. Staff members at all tiers of student services have been empowered through information to assist students more readily and completely.

An assessment of the Front Door Center, conducted by the Center for Applied Research at Central Piedmont Community College (2009), showed that the first point of contact was smoother than before, the enrollment process was streamlined, and student satisfaction with the process had improved. The study validated the college's using student feedback to facilitate policy change. Although some positions did not require cross-training for the three different areas, the staff in all three areas reported that they were more knowledgeable about processes and procedures in the other areas. Silos have been taken down.

GTCC employed a holistic approach that provided intellectual development for all levels of staff, disseminated the student-centered philosophy, and provided the physical proximity of services that students needed. This was an unsettling approach at first, but by courageously addressing students' needs rather than continuing an ineffective institutional tradition, GTCC implemented a smoother enrollment process and increased student satisfaction.

The key component to the success of this initiative was cross-training employees in the admissions, records, and financial aid services. GTCC committed appropriate focus, dollars, and time in the initial stages of the reorganization. Furthermore, it continues this commitment by establishing procedures for ongoing training in customer service, computer and database use, and the nuances of the services available to the students at the front door.

LESSONS LEARNED

- Make a commitment to act. Consider what will happen to your institution if no action is taken. As you and your colleagues become aware of the important issue of leadership development, take steps to learn what to do and how to do it. Invest resources, even in lean financial times, to prepare leaders in all areas of the college. And, as we always do in community colleges, start with a committee or task force! The task force will provide a wide range of ideas, ownership of the process, and illustrate to the college community the importance of leadership throughout the college.
- Community colleges face enormous challenges in an increasingly complex and rapidly changing environment. Couple this with a greater level of upcoming

retirements, and there is an increasing sense of urgency to have well-prepared leaders throughout the college.

- Employee development is a partnership between the college and each employee. This partnership is an investment by the employee and the college that pays off in job enrichment, personal growth, and increased effectiveness for both the employee and the college.

- By providing opportunities for growth and development, all employees can grow and improve and broaden their knowledge, skills, and abilities. Leaders throughout the college community, including the board of trustees, faculty, administrators, staff, and students, need to develop an appreciation for what can be achieved by participating in a systemic, integrated, continual process rather than sporadic, disparate professional development programs.

- The college environment must be a cultural fabric that weaves together the contribution of all employees in an atmosphere of trust, calculated risk-taking, and value-added participation in leadership.

One LEAD graduate summarized leadership at GTCC as follows:

> Leadership does not always require that one be out front, but instead that one possess the skills to be positive, caring, fair, understanding, and reliable. Leadership also requires that one possess the character and integrity to shepherd a group of people to a higher level of attainment. Effective leadership requires a commitment to be the best and to expect the best from yourself and those around you.

REFERENCES

Buck, J., & MacGregor, F. (2001, March). Preparing future faculty: A faculty-in-training pilot program. *Teaching English in the two-year college, 28*(3), 241–250.

Cameron, D. W. (2010, January). *GTCC succession planning management toolkit.* Greensboro, NC: Guilford Technical Community College.

Center for Applied Research. (2009, June). *Five-year summative evaluation of the Achieving the Dream initiative for Guilford Technical Community College.* Charlotte, NC: Central Piedmont Community College.

Greenlee, J. (2008). *Succession planning management toolkit.* Greensboro, NC: Guilford Technical Community College.

Rothwell, W. J. (2010, October 3). *Succession planning in higher education* [Webinar]. Austin, TX: The University of Texas System Leadership Institute.

Weisman, I. M., & Vaughan, G. B. (2007). *The community college presidency: 2006* (AACC-RB-07-1). Washington, DC: American Association of Community Colleges.

CHAPTER 3

Pursuing Student Success

John E. Roueche and Suanne D. Roueche

The Challenge:
Ensuring that the open door to community college is not a revolving door.

The Response:
Embracing a culture of change throughout the college that places student success at the heart of all programs and initiatives.

If your actions inspire others to dream more, learn more,

do more, and become more, you are a leader.

—John Quincy Adams

COMMUNITY COLLEGES IN THE NATIONAL STUDENT SUCCESS SPOTLIGHT

n December 2008, the Bill & Melinda Gates Foundation launched a long-term funding initiative, the Developmental Education Initiative (DEI), with the goal of doubling the number of low-income adults who, by age 26, earn a college degree or credential that meets job-market demands. In July 2009, President Obama challenged community colleges to produce another 5 million graduates by 2020 in the American Graduation Initiative (White House, 2009). In April 2010, the American Association of Community Colleges and five other organizations (Association of Community College Trustees, Center for Community College Student Engagement (CCCSE), League for Innovation in the Community College, National Institute for Staff and Organizational Development, and Phi Theta Kappa) issued a "call to action," a commitment to produce 50% more students with high-quality degrees and certificates (degrees and certificates deemed to be of value to the job market) by 2020. Also in April 2010, Lumina Foundation announced Goal 2025, calling for increasing the proportion of Americans with high-quality degrees and credentials to 60% by 2025 (Lumina Foundation, 2012). In response, state boards and community colleges around the nation have been approving strategic plans and launching initiatives to double the number of credential recipients by 2020, including transfer-bound students.

The national completion agenda has put community colleges in the spotlight they have long wished for—to be recognized as the nation's best hope for providing the education and skills its citizens need to keep the economy strong into the future. Unfortunately, that same spotlight exposes some glaring realities of the current situation community colleges are in. Current data warn community colleges that their work is still cut out for them, as it has been for some time.

Challenge #1: Finding New Resources to Keep the Doors Open

The national college completion agenda significantly increases the effort and, as a result, the funds needed to improve completion rates. As enrollment numbers increase and funding decreases, many colleges are finding it a challenge to keep their doors open. To accommodate more students, colleges must enhance faculty, programs, and facilities at the same time that the resources to meet demand are dwindling.

The magnitude of these problems, especially as they affect those less able to pay these increases, cannot be ignored or denied. The College Board (2011) reported that, in 2010, public 2-year colleges charged an average of $2,963 for tuition, up 8.7% over the previous year's average and double the inflation rate of 3.6% between July 2010 and 2011. At the same time, family earnings dropped across all income levels and state funding per student declined by 4% in 2010. The hopes that financial aid will improve are dashed by statistics showing that state-funded student aid is not expected to keep up with tuition increases. "High tuition/high aid only works if student aid rises every time tuition is raised. This is not happening now" (Katsinas, D'Amico, & Friedel, 2011, p. 6).

As Mullin (2010) reported in *Doing More With Less: The Inequitable Funding of Community Colleges,* community colleges "have not received a fair share of funding in light of their role in the country's higher education systems" and "improvements in the delivery of community college education cannot overcome the stark reality of inadequate funding" (p. 4). "Surging enrollments at community colleges over the past two years have not been met with proportional increases in fiscal support, placing community colleges across the country in the position of doing more with less, or, in some cases, simply doing less" (p. 5). The report portends a new category of students, "idle assets"—students who might benefit from higher education but are in effect denied access to community colleges that are negatively affected by cuts in appropriations.

Because community colleges look to federal, state, and local governments and federal agencies for the bulk of their support, current trends of continuing decreases in those funds will make the 50% increase in productivity on the current national political agenda difficult to achieve. Mullin (2010) also stated: "Community colleges received just 27% of total federal, state, and local revenues (operating and nonoperating) for public degree-granting institutions in 2007–2008 while serving 43% of undergraduate students" (p. 4). In addition, community colleges have historically received only 20% of state tax appropriations and considerably fewer federal funds than other sectors of higher education. One consequence is that many of the "idle asset" students could be sitting in the classrooms of much-needed programs, such as nursing and allied health, where community colleges are the leading producers of graduates—50% of all new nurses are community college graduates (National Commission on Community Colleges, 2008).

Challenge #2: Serving a Highly Diverse Student Population

Those who enroll in community college are a highly diverse population along every demographic dimension (e.g., age, race/ethnicity, socioeconomic status, employment status, and academic preparedness). As a result, colleges are challenged to provide an increasing variety of support services to enable students to meet their goals. Colleges must identify strategies for helping students focus on their academic work while performing remarkable juggling acts as they attempt to balance work, family, and financial responsibilities. By identifying ways to help them achieve better balance, colleges improve academic outcomes. Students' realities require that colleges understand better what they need, what barriers they must address and overcome, and what support structures must be institutionalized to make success possible.

At the same time, colleges must not allow the enormous challenges that students bring with them to lower the expectations that either party has for their success. As community college educator Vincent Tinto observed: "No one rises to low expectations" (cited in Marklein, 2008). High expectations generally encourage more effort, raise performance levels, and increase motivation and tenacity necessary for doing better.

Challenge #3: Stopping the Revolving Door

Not all students who attend community colleges have a goal of earning a degree or certificate. To analyze effectiveness, colleges need to identify who these students are and why they attend. Of greater concern, however, is that of those students who do intend to obtain a credential, a great number leave before doing so. The open door too frequently becomes a revolving door. Only 28% of first-time, full-time, associate degree-seeking community college students graduate with a certificate or an associate degree within 3 years. Only slightly more than half of first-time, full-time public community college students return for their second year (CCCSE, 2010, pp. 3–4).

Data confirm a sizable gap between the percentage of students who set and meet a completion goal: Fewer than half of all students with a goal of earning a community college degree or certificate will have met their goal 6 years later (CCCSE, 2010, p. 5). Other data indicate that while enrollment in community colleges is increasing "at more than three times the rate of four-year colleges … retention at community colleges is slipping fast … only 30 percent of students entering community college graduate in six years" (Larose, n.d.).

Challenge #4: Assessing and Documenting Success Accurately and Meaningfully

To document success in terms of the national completion agenda, community colleges are expected to collect and report data using existing systems that do not capture the uniqueness of the community college model. For example, completion is currently universally measured in terms of credentials earned, which means that students who complete community college courses without the intention to earn a credential are essentially counted as noncompleters, even though they have met their goals. Another dimension that existing systems inadequately capture is workforce preparedness. That is, colleges must stay true to the critical goal of awarding degrees and certificates that have market value. They must ensure that graduates' skill and knowledge levels are commensurate with employers' expectations, that they are prepared to fill the positions they seek, are prepared for transfer to a 4-year institution, and are performing reasonably well at the next academic levels.

The work of improving completion rates has a built-in admonition and warning. As O'Banion observed: "Great movements … often have unintended consequences, and it would be wise for all of us to consider what these consequences might be for the completion agenda. We must ask the question: 'To what end?'" (2010, p. 45). There must be documentable links between what learning occurs and what completion means. If we are successful in awarding more degrees but we can determine that less learning has occurred or that the learning has no significant value in the marketplace— either for students seeking to continue in higher education or those seeking skills needed for immediate employment—then higher graduation rates do not necessarily spell success. Completion must mean something better for students, changing their lives and, by design, improving the state of our economy and the quality of our collective future.

Furthermore, community colleges need to come to a consensus about what being "college-ready" really means, especially as we shift parameters with various assessment cut-off test scores and make academic advising decisions based upon potentially life-changing numbers. Colleges need assessment tools and strategies to establish better cause–effect relationships between what they assess; what they predict will occur as a result of that assessment if an appropriate, recommended academic path is not taken; and how that information actually relates to subsequent educational performance.

Decades after publication of *The Nation at Risk* (National Commission on Excellence in Education, 1983), which called upon colleges to increase accountability for student progress and success, colleges are again being called upon to do so. Although progress is being made to assess and document success through initiatives such as the Voluntary Framework of Accountability (AACC, 2012), accountability measures appropriate for assessing success at community colleges are yet to be defined and implemented. The imperative to capture and report data is especially difficult for community colleges already struggling with constrained budgets and insufficient IT infrastructure.

There is some cautious optimism that the colleges selected to receive funds from the $2 billion Trade Adjustment Assistance Community College and Career Training (TAACCCT) program will be helped significantly. In the first of four funding cycles slated for FY 2011–2014, of 32 grants awarded, 23 went to multi-institutional consortia and 9 to single institutions. The average grant size was approximately $214 million. Although the activities funded varied widely, most of the grants already awarded focused on colleges providing training in specific fields such as health care and aerospace and to those providing adult basic and developmental education, with a focus on attaining credentials (J. Hermes, personal communication, 2012).

Challenge #5: Improving Academic Preparedness

The large majority of first-time entering students—more than 60% by most estimates—test into one or more developmental courses (Bailey, 2009); a sizable proportion of those testing into these courses never enroll in them, fail them, drop out of them, or drop out without even failing (Bailey, Jeong, & Cho, 2010). Of those students who do complete required developmental courses, small percentages are successful in completing them, and even smaller percentages enroll subsequently in college-level courses and perform successfully in reasonable time periods.

The pervasive view is that the large majority of developmental programs accomplish little (Bailey & Cho, 2010). Achieving the Dream (ATD) Director Byron McClenney argues, "the most significant thing is to invest in developmental education as a college and to do it unapologetically and with high expectations" (personal communication, 2011). Including part-time students taking developmental courses in the accounting of all students' performance would fuel a more alarming response to current student success reports.

THE ELEPHANT IN THE ROOM: DEVELOPMENTAL EDUCATION

The most daunting challenge community colleges face may be improving students' academic preparedness for college-level course work. The reality is that little has been accomplished in developmental education programs and strategies over many years, and community colleges continue to seek answers to questions about why it is so difficult to create successful programs that can provide instruction in basic skills to help achieve desirable student success levels.

Research on Developmental Education

For more than 40 years, we have studied how community colleges have responded to the large numbers of students entering their doors unprepared academically for college work. Although colleges' responses to developmental education have been mixed over the last two decades, there has been no scarcity of programmatic models that hold promise for improving outcomes for and responding to the academic challenges posed by academically underprepared students. Numerous researchers have kept the spotlight on developmental education; their work is familiar to community college professionals who have long been grappling with the dilemma of balancing the open-door and academic excellence missions. Three areas of research include learning communities, success strategies, and best practices.

Learning Communities

Vincent Tinto, a professor at Syracuse University, has conducted significant research on student retention and the impact of learning communities on student growth and attainment. He can arguably be credited for proposing that the "fit" between students and colleges is the most critical determiner of whether students leave or stay. In *Leaving College: Rethinking the Causes and Cures of Student Attrition,* Tinto (1994) argued persuasively that students who are more involved in the college, both academically and through extracurricular activities, are more likely to stay.

Building on that concept, he further proposed that the learning community approach was especially key to retaining underprepared students (Tinto, 1998). His work showcased colleges that had been successful with this approach, and those examples of success resonated with many, including GTCC. The primary characteristics of learning communities are block scheduling that keeps cohorts of students together, which facilitates study teams, and courses that are linked by a theme, content, or discipline. Although every learning community is unique, according to the purpose for which it is created, common to all learning communities is that they are designed to promote the sharing of knowledge and experience among the members of the cohort.

Success Strategies

Success strategies and best practices are current terms to describe administrative and instructional behaviors, policies, programs, and protocols that appear to work in helping students succeed. Ending late registration, using call centers to keep in touch with students who are absent from classes, and requiring mentors for at-risk students are all practices that many colleges have found to make a positive difference in performance outcomes.

CCCSE's feedback data from students responding to questions about how engaged they are with their college, how they perceive the college is engaged with them, and so on, provide colleges with valuable information about student retention (and potential attrition). These data apply to all students and are especially poignant as they relate to the most at-risk students who are most likely to leave a college when circumstances in which they are uncomfortable or complicated present themselves. Some of the practices that colleges begin to consider with these data in hand also can be referred to as "promising practices"—"strategies that appear to be associated with a variety of indicators of student progress and success" (CCCSE, 2012).

Hunter Boylan, director of the National Center for Developmental Education (NCDE), is one of the premier researchers in the field of developmental education and continues to identify and disseminate research-based best-practice models for successful developmental programming. In *What Works: Research-Based Best Practices in Developmental Education,* Boylan (2002) presents the results of national studies of promising benchmarks. Boylan observed that the guide identifies practically everything we know from research on how to design, implement, and evaluate developmental education and learning assistance programs, including topics such as effective organization, classroom techniques, program evaluation, and support services. This research of theory and practice arguably represent the most useful compendium of proven practice to inform development of existing programs.

Of special interest is the updated inventory of practices that any college may use to evaluate its own developmental program, measuring the extent to which its program represents the most promising and best practices as reported in the study. The results of a careful rating of a college's own program practices against those reported in the study could provide a fertile field for setting priorities for program and instructional change.

The ATD initiative assists colleges to design and implement student success strategies that are proven to make a positive difference in student retention numbers. The steps to effective developmental education that ATD director McClenney has articulated reiterate earlier-drawn conclusions about developmental education but also reinforce the best thinking and most promising practices for improved student retention and success that have emerged from research.

Achieving the Dream: Community Colleges Count

ATD is a major national initiative launched in 2003, designed to improve educational outcomes for community college students, particularly low-income and students of color. ATD leaders have been studying and coaching community colleges toward improved student performance and completion rates successfully, using appropriate institutional data from which to craft and implement a viable student success agenda. ATD's ultimate aim is to create a "culture of evidence" on college campuses that drives the creation and implementation of strategies that, if data-informed and implemented purposefully, will improve student outcomes.

ATD coaches help colleges lay the groundwork for and encourage ongoing "courageous conversations" from which college stakeholders emerge to make appropriate changes to their current systems, while maintaining high levels of responsibility and accountability for promoting institutional transformative change that can improve student performance and increase completion rates. Drawing from more than 1,200 reports prepared by the 33 members of the ATD coaching cadre during 6 years of college and intensive work, ATD leaders identified the 10 foundational steps most essential to an institution's making progress with its own transformation to improve student success (see Table 3.1). ATD colleges are encouraged to take proactive steps toward gathering appropriate data, to analyze and use the data to drive informed policy decisions and implementation strategies, and to assess institutional effectiveness specifically.

Table 3.1: Top Ten Reasons for Progress in Achieving the Dream

1. Leaders, including board members and faculty, are engaged in, and pay continuous attention to, progress on the student success agenda.

2. A sustained focus on student success is practiced by the institution and demonstrably influences the development of policies, procedures, and practices.

3. There is broad and continuous faculty/staff/student/community engagement and collaboration in support of a student success agenda.

4. Planning and budgeting (including reallocation of resources) are aligned with vision, priorities, and strategies of a student success agenda.

5. A culture of evidence and inquiry is pervasive in the institution (including cohort tracking of disaggregated data) with strong support from IR.

6. A sense of urgency drives a shared vision and communications around a student success agenda with internal and external stakeholders.

7. Professional development efforts (inclusive of board members, CEO, leadership throughout the institution, full-time and adjunct faculty, and staff) are aligned with priorities and strategies of a student success agenda.

8. A systemic student success agenda is integrated with other significant initiatives such as accreditation, strategic planning, and Title V.

9. An equity agenda is integrated in the efforts to improve learning and college completion outcomes.

10. Student success interventions are informed by and adapted from demonstrably effective practices.

Note. Reprinted with permission from McClenney (2010).

Colleges applying for ATD grant funds must work to improve overall student success rates as measured by these five indicators:

1. Completion of developmental education courses.
2. Completion of introductory-level, or gatekeeper, college courses.
3. Completion of courses with a C or higher.
4. Persistence from term to term and year to year.
5. Attainment of a degree or certificate.

In return, each ATD college receives support from two consultants: a data facilitator, who helps the college with data processing and management, and a coach, who assists college leaders as they move forward with their student success agenda.

To better align external and internal support, colleges must create two committees to guide their efforts under the ATD initiative: a core team responsible for overseeing decision making about programs and resource allocation, and a data team responsible for analyzing and disseminating student outcomes data. Additionally, several professional development opportunities are provided through an annual Strategy

Institute and Web-based seminars where colleges meet and share information about progress and challenges.

Grants of up to $450,000 are available for colleges making a 5-year commitment to ATD. When colleges apply for an ATD grant, they agree to be mentored through an institution-wide five-step improvement process, as follows:

1. Commit to institutional reform aimed at improving student success rates.
2. Analyze data on student outcomes in order to identify barriers to student achievement and prioritize areas for reform.
3. Engage a broad base of stakeholders in developing strategies to address priority problems.
4. Implement, evaluate, and improve student success strategies.
5. Institutionalize and scale up effective policies and practices.

In its latest report, published January 2011, CCRC researchers described the future promise of the ATD model as follows:

> While larger changes in students' achievement may not yet have been realized, Achieving the Dream has begun an unprecedented movement toward helping colleges improve their student outcomes and develop systems to sustain those efforts. Bringing faculty and staff voices more concretely into colleges' reform work and focusing more directly on improvements to classroom instruction and services may reap benefits for the next stage of the initiative's work. Given the successes they have already had, the initiative and its participating colleges stand poised to move forward with this agenda and make the changes needed to help more community college students accomplish their goals. (Rutschow et al., 2011, pp. ES13–14)

Fostering Institution-Wide Commitment to Student Success

Research indicates that less than one quarter of all students earn a degree within 3 years of enrolling in a community college. Students' own efforts can only take them so far, and the multiple challenges of family, work, poor academic preparation, in combination with classroom expectations and demands can take them off the academic playing field. The college has to address these issues by being proactive in helping level the playing field for everyone. The responsibility for addressing issues that are beyond what students can achieve by their own efforts is shared by everyone at the college, but especially by the board, president, administrators, and faculty.

ATD encourages colleges to address this joint responsibility through regular information sharing, beginning at the highest levels, to signal buy-in and to send a message to the entire college family that this work is critical to the institution's well-being. The college community looks to the board to test the reliability and veracity of the institution's message about its real goals and objectives, its real values and serious concerns, its real commitment to "walking its talk." Leadership is key to setting the stage, to sharing the vision, to promoting a culture that speaks to total buy-in to the concept of student success and to institutional designs and policies that support it. The board, at the top of that institutional leadership pyramid, is the single entity that speaks loud and clear when it articulates its commitment to answering the difficult questions about college performance.

Peter Ewell is vice president of the National Center for Higher Education Management Systems (NCHEMS), a research and development center established to help colleges and universities improve management effectiveness. Ewell has offered clear, realistic advice on the board's role in overseeing the most important business of the academic side of the house—educating students. As a recognized authority in the field of board trends in assessment and management of academic programs, or what boards can do to ensure academic quality, his advice provides some important lessons for community colleges looking to send a clear message about this important business.

In *Making the Grade: How Boards Can Ensure Academic Quality* (2006), Ewell posed numerous questions that, while more typically asked by boards of directors in other settings, particularly in for-profit business sectors, could help colleges "define the territory," address the "quality assurance" issues, and get a better picture of the quality and value of the college's teaching and learning functions. He has recommended that these questions (see Table 3.2) be addressed and answered in educational settings, beginning at the highest levels of leadership, with those who have the bird's-eye view of the institution and responsibility for overseeing and assessing the business of educating students—the college's most important products. These questions are at the heart of addressing institutional goals that support student success, and when asked in the interest of getting accurate answers about performance, they drive home the collective agreement that student success is an institutional priority of the highest order.

Increasing interest in academic excellence, in "value added" to individuals and to communities, goes far beyond the basic issue of accreditation as the most important seal of approval. Putting monitoring devices in place, such as regular data collection processes to gather answers to questions about behaviors and results that "matter," is important work to accomplish and to have ready answers to questions from stakeholders and data to substantiate requests for support at any level. We are reminded that boards have fine lines to walk between playing their roles relative to "strategic direction" and fiduciary responsibilities, and avoiding overstepping their boundaries and intruding into the roles played by others in tending to the "details of how things should be done." They must practice patience with the sometimes seemingly interminable deliberations and processes on the academic side of the college house, and remain committed—in spite of the annoying delays posed by the time-consuming work of defining and describing "value" and "performance" and "progress"—to asking critical assessment questions about the work of the institution.

The Community College Research Center (CCRC) has been studying ATD colleges since the initiative began. In their 2009 report, *Building Student Success From the Ground Up: A Case Study of an Achieving the Dream College,* CCRC researchers Elizabeth Zachry and Genevieve Orr observed: "Since joining Achieving the Dream, Guilford has transformed into a data-driven, success-oriented institution focused on systemic efforts to improve student achievement" (p. ES-1). Many of the practices described in recent research are reflected in GTCC's initiatives, including organization, instructional techniques, evaluation strategies, and support services that characterize its ATD-related developmental education program initiatives.

In implementing strategies and practices resulting from its ATD initiatives, GTCC's board, administrators, and faculty recognized GTCC as a learner-centered college. But

Table 3.2: Aligning Institutional Processes With the Student Success Agenda: A Model for Community College Leaders	
Key Questions for Community College Leaders	**Institutional Process**
1. How Good Is Your Product? Your principal product is student learning; therefore, the quality of learning outcomes should be of central concern to the college. The ultimate indicator of the quality of the product is what a student knows and can do upon graduation. The process of producing the product is instruction. Value is added to the product through instruction when students know more and can do more upon graduation than they could before entering the institution.	Assess student learning outcomes.
2. How Good Are You at Producing Your Product? The only way you can answer this question is to monitor the patterns of the students entering and leaving the institution. These patterns affect costs and outcomes.	Monitor student retention and graduation rates.
3. Are Your Customers Satisfied? Your customers include your current students as well as other key stakeholders: prospective students, students' parents, employers, civic opinion leaders, and the general community.	Examine the perceptions and opinions of stakeholders to tailor your product and anticipate emerging needs.
4. Do You Have the Right Mix of Products? To ensure that the college offers graduate-level products in demand in the marketplace, you need to periodically take stock of what's in your product portfolio.	Conduct academic program reviews.
5. Do You Make the Grade? Accreditation is a basic certification of quality and is critical to maintain for your college to remain in good standing.	Maintain institutional accreditation.
Note. Adapted from Ewell (2006, pp. viii–ix).	

quickly into discussions of its developing success agenda, college leaders across the institution realized that without reliable data, collected and analyzed on a regular basis, any changes to instruction and student services were ill-informed and, therefore, ill-advised. Hence, the leaders of the institution took the proverbial bull by the horns, and the student success pieces of the puzzle begin to fall into place. GTCC ultimately limited its learning community efforts specifically to students in developmental and transitional courses, recognizing the value of themed collaborative approaches as a strategy for keeping those students engaged and focused.

A satisfied customer is like a walking billboard ... By exceeding people's expectations you make a statement—*their needs come first*. All of us feel good when something like that happens in our lives ... Imagine what would happen if a college ... began to exceed the expectations of its customers—employers, students, alumni, parents, board members, state legislators, local community members. Imagine the stories that would be told and retold. (Seymour, 1993, p. 179)

GTCC'S STUDENT SUCCESS AGENDA

Effecting a Culture of Change

GTCC has tackled its student success issues from a position of strength, drawing directly from some of the most proactive work being accomplished under the banner and mantra of institutional transformation for the purposes of improving student success. GTCC aligned the college with promising efforts to identify problems and solutions and took on initiatives that were potential paths to transforming the culture and the outcome data. Most notably, in 2004, GTCC joined the ranks of colleges working on the ATD initiative and subsequently participated in the DEI, to expand small or pilot programs that have shown some promise. The entire college has embraced the idea of looking at its effectiveness and implementing data-informed initiatives, all generated by its commitment to identifying appropriate interventions where institutional policy, programs, and student needs intersect.

We have learned that change that is "anchored in cultural change" (Massey & Hart, 2010, p. 7) will provide the best chance to establish and effect long-lasting and sustainable change. But for cultural change to occur and prosper, it must begin at the top: Presidents and their leadership teams are the best coaches for the change process, getting others interested, then involved, then taking the reins of its growth and development.

Cameron and two trustees—Shirley Frye and David Miller—served on the college's ATD Core Team. Their participation was identified as a significant first step in changing the college's culture. Kathryn Baker Smith, who led ATD at GTCC for 5 years as vice president of educational support services (now retired), observed "Their presence let people know that Achieving the Dream was important to the leadership of the college" (ATD, 2010, p. 2). The result of the trustees' requests that she report to them, on a quarterly basis, about the progress of ATD strategies was that the entire board became a secondary core team. "Now student success issues, not just decisions about bricks and mortar, are regular agenda items for GTCC trustees," Smith said (ATD, 2010, p. 2).

Engaging Faculty

The role of faculty in the student success agenda is the linchpin of the enterprise. Without their commitment, support, and involvement, there is little hope that change will occur. GTCC engaged faculty in the success agenda early on, with the intent of spreading a culture of evidence across campuses and classrooms. In accordance with ATD guidelines, GTCC established a data team, the Learning Evidence Committee, composed of rotating members, including vice presidents, administrators, division chairs, faculty, and staff. This committee continues to serve as a review and advising body for the institutional resources (IR) department. Faculty and staff members rotate out of appointments every 2 years, thereby increasing the number of personnel who work closely with institutional performance data, as well as with data specific to ATD strategies. The committee has played a major role in attending to collected data—analyzing it and then disseminating the findings to the college at large.

With the help of the IR director, the committee created GTCC's institutional scorecard to strengthen the college's focus on tracking student outcomes. The scorecard was designed to graphically depict the written goals for student achievement and engagement and institutional progress. Indicators of student success include successful course completion, graduation, fall-to-fall persistence, progression from developmental to higher-level courses, satisfaction for employers and students, and enrollment growth. Target ranges for each of the indicators then measure the college's actual performance and its progress in meeting target goals each year. For example, if a particular target range is met, or is not, the college may decide to increase its target goals for the next year, or conversely, look for ways to improve its performance and meet the goal in a subsequent year.

The committee subsequently established data-based decision-making as a major commitment for the entire college family. As the value of the scorecard became more obvious as institutional strategic planning and budget process tools, other scorecards were created at the division and the department levels in all academic areas. Those could be tailored for specific academic areas and thereby pique the interest of faculty and staff not yet fully committed data collection and analysis. Results of the committee's efforts to date include significant increases in faculty requests for reports on student performance in classes and programs, as well as departmental and program reports and in requests for help in developing their own research studies (e.g., to test new instructional methods). These requests signal a significant trend toward improved and increasing data collection, analysis, application, and implementation of new strategies.

Professional development at GTCC has increasingly focused on student success. Faculty and staff are invited to participate in strategy development, implementation, assessment, and refining courses and programs. Early on, more than half of the first year's ATD grant money was dedicated to professional development for faculty and staff. For example, faculty and staff were able to visit other colleges piloting interventions of interest to GTCC—intake procedures at Valencia Community College (FL) and learning communities at Evergreen State College (WA). This kind of professional development opportunity helps GTCC avoid expending scarce funds on reinventing the wheel.

Addressing the Greatest Needs and Widest Gaps

Convinced that the college could do better by all students and improve its student success numbers, GTCC turned to looking at the evidence that would identify achievement gaps. As were other ATD colleges, GTCC was encouraged to look at its own unique, specific student needs, set priorities for addressing them, identify strategies for addressing each priority, and then begin an implementation phase during which they were to pilot new interventions and programs. Within a year of its initial planning phase (2004–2005), GTCC had expanded its services to focus on addressing significant retention problem areas as identified in the two critical, most at-risk target student populations—developmental education students and first-year students.

In analyzing data from a variety of sources, GTCC recognized significant needs to improve retention, course completion, and graduation rates for all students; however, students needing remediation, minority students, male students (especially minority male students), and students younger than 25 years of age, were especially in need of focused attention to improve their performance and GTCC's student success outcome data. While GTCC employed multiple strategies across the colleges to meeting its ATD goals, the strategies we report here were especially productive and are, therefore, promising strategies that would be subjects for future data analysis. Board members and top-level administrators continued to support college efforts to improve its condition. The message remained consistent, board meeting by board meeting, Learning Evidence Committee meeting by meeting.

Supplemental Instruction
GTCC launched its supplemental instruction (SI) program in spring 2007, as a voluntary walk-in option for students enrolled in the introductory algebra developmental math course. SI is an academic assistance program that offers regularly scheduled peer-assisted study sessions and walk-in assistance with homework, deciphering lecture notes, developing organizational tools, and integrating course content and study skills. The SI coordinator is responsible for identifying the targeted course, gaining faculty support, selecting and training SI leaders, and evaluating the program. Developmental math faculty screen SI leaders—students who have been deemed course competent,

approved by the SI coordinator and the course instructor, and excel in proactive learning and study strategies. SI leaders attend course lectures, take notes, complete assigned material, and conduct three to five out-of-class SI sessions a week. The SI is the "model student," a facilitator who helps students to integrate course content and learning/study strategies.

Outcome data have shown that SI students tend to remain in the course throughout the semester and have higher success and completion rates (Center for Applied Research, 2009). Further study results may indicate that SI is in fact a methodology that could be used to close the success gap for students with initially low math placement scores or those repeating developmental math. Success data led GTCC to change the status of this program from voluntary to mandatory, requiring attendance in a one-hour weekly session that is attached to selected sections of the introductory algebra course.

SOAR: New Student Orientation

A new student orientation program began fall 2005. Previously the college had held a one-hour orientation session for new students. This orientation initiative was implemented as a result of input from students and faculty concerned that new students needed more information. Orientation was expanded to approximately 3 hours and included general information, academic success strategies, and academic planning. Student orientation began as voluntary for students but was highly encouraged by staff.

These participants were evenly distributed among academic placement categories. The persistent theme in the participant evaluations was the desire to register for classes at the end of orientation. Due to the participant feedback, advising and registration was added as the last session during orientation, and the event became known as Student Orientation, Advising, and Registration (SOAR).

SOAR is now a mandatory 3-hour credit-bearing course for all new students. It is exceeding its fall-to-fall persistence goal, even for the most at-risk student population: minority men. Early on, even as a voluntary course, this initiative was reaching an extraordinarily large number of students and demonstrated increasing persistence percentages. Analysis indicated (Center for Applied Research, 2009) there were statistically significant differences in persistence between students who attended SOAR and those who did not, but causation was not implied by the analysis. When SOAR was not required, some argued that only the more motivated students attended SOAR and that high motivation levels could have accounted for the differences. They might have been right; faculty acknowledged that more academically prepared students tended to skip SOAR. Now that SOAR is mandatory, more analyses of this trend will provide better results. In all, SOAR continued to exceed its goal of achieving fall-to-fall persistence rates of greater than 51%, even for minority men. During the DEI grant year, some new components for developmental education students (those needing two or more developmental courses) were added. A specialized SOAR began summer 2009.

Split Math Program

GTCC piloted its split math program in fall 2005 in an effort to improve the success rate and within-course retention of developmental math students. The program targeted students with the greatest risk of failing; who started in the lowest level developmental math course; who earned a C in the next level developmental math course; and who were repeating the third-level course. The course was split into two parts, which allowed students to complete in two semesters and effectively slowed the pace of the course for those students who had difficulty completing it in the one-semester framework. The instructor teaching this pilot course reported that many students overcame their fear of math and developed some confidence in their math abilities. The students appeared more relaxed because they felt there would be time to absorb the new information. They were very supportive of each other, and some developed study groups that met outside of class (Center for Applied Research, 2009).

The program was repeated in fall 2006, with similar results. Both the fall 2005 and 2006 cohorts showed higher success rates in the course, higher retention, and higher persistence into subsequent terms. Averaged together, split math students persisted into the next term at a significantly higher rate and to the following fall at a higher rate than GTCC's fall-to-fall persistence rates, with success data reporting in at college completion rates for the original cohort (Center for Applied Research, 2009).

However, the structure of the program was not aligned with the common course library, and an appeal to the state system office to continue this project was denied. The program seems promising, at least for a specific group of at-risk students. GTCC's final reports indicated that it was time to take the success, persistence, and graduation results to the system office and seek approval to offer split math in a format that appears to be worthy of consideration, with short- and long-term promising results. Success indicators were that two cohorts of students included in this project showed higher success rates in the split math course, higher retention, and higher persistence into subsequent terms.

Minority Male Mentoring Program

A male mentoring program began spring 2006, with a target population of minority male students who were underperforming academically (were in one or more developmental courses, first-generation college goers, or GED/adult high school attendees). The program was called Brothers Relating Opportunities for Success (BROS; GTCC, 2011). All students participating in this program were assigned a faculty or staff male mentor, encouraged to meet with the mentor at least twice a month, and asked to attend one success strategies luncheon each month. The goal was to improve the term-to-term persistence. This program met with encouraging success and was deemed worthy of continuing in future semesters.

Developmental Learning Community

GTCC instructors who had been teaching developmental English courses for several years and had followed students who placed into the lowest level for language skills had noticed that course completion rates were predictably low and persistence rates even lower. Academic deficiencies were compounded by family, financial, and work-related issues. In response, in fall 2005, GTCC began offering a "linked-course" option.

All students who enrolled in developmental English, a 4-day-a-week course, also enrolled in a student success course offered at the same time on the fifth day. The course covered topics that often present barriers to these students: time management, study skills, and learning styles. Students spent a good portion of the semester on goal setting and completion. The major project for the semester was to choose one realistic goal, create a plan for achieving it, and to present the success or failure of achieving that goal as the final exam. In addition, students participated in career exploration; took reality checks to assess personal abilities, preferences, and long-term goals; explored offerings at GTCC and beyond to find achievable, reasonable career options in fields that they may not have thought of previously; and learned to manage college to meet the new goals. Students taking this linked-course option improved remarkably, and term-to-term retention improved. Moreover, results suggested that this strategy was especially beneficial for Black male students.

College Study Skills Courses

GTCC identified a need to improve success and persistence in its paralegal and office systems technology (OST) gateway courses. The idea was that persistence would improve if students became engaged with the program instructors early in their GTCC experience. As a result, as of 2005, GTCC began offering "College Study Skills," a one credit-hour course designed to increase the new student's preparation for college. Students review learning styles, time management skills, college resources, goal setting, career awareness, and other items specific to each student's selected program of study. The course was expanded to include information technology courses in 2006.

Data comparing students who took the study skills course in conjunction with the OST gateway course indicate that they were more likely to complete the gateway course than were students enrolled in the prior year. Data on Black male students were even more striking: The first-term persistence rate for these students was 85%, compared with 65% for those not taking the course (Center for Applied Research, 2009). Those data sparked a wide-ranging discussion of how the study skills course might be effective with other students, particularly underserved and at-risk students. Consequently, all programs in GTCC's business technologies division began requiring this course.

A second 3-contact-hour study skills course was designed to focus on affective as well as academic skills. Based on the success of the original study skills course, GTCC was selected to participate in a rigorous random assignment study to look at the potential of a larger effort that would generate the same positive trends. As of 2009, as described in the Center for Applied Research's report relative to GTCC's 5-year progress report, this course was not living up to expectations, and concerns were expressed about the program and control groups. Further study has been indicated, especially investigating the possibility that if the course were required, students would be more likely to stay long enough to gain the effects for which the course was intended—to improve persistence and retention. The structured study indicated a need to target the course and its content to the college's culture and to particular groups of students. Work continues.

The Transitions Learning Community

The Transitions Learning Community (TLC) was created as a strategy for helping developmental reading students transition into college-level course work. Correlating developmental reading grades with grades in targeted subsequent courses—music, psychology, sociology, and English—indicated that students who had a grade of C struggled in subsequent courses, more so than those with higher grades and those who placed out of reading. Based on this analysis, those students were invited to take part in TLC, which began in fall 2005 and included a student success course, expository writing, writing lab, and general psychology.

This project was designed to provide an academic setting where students who have successfully completed developmental reading course sequences can get support as they learn to transfer skills to curriculum courses. Instructors meet regularly outside of class time to share overviews of courses and to discuss details of how to coordinate and link activities and assignments. Students learn to interact with diverse course content, instructors, and peers. Ideally, TLC provides academic support and counseling.

Students are recruited for the TLC from the developmental reading classes during the semester prior to pre-registration. Brochures are distributed, questions are answered, and interested students sign up. The lead instructors check each student's qualifications (prerequisites and previous course work), call them, and explain the sign-up process at registration. The courses are capped at 20 students. The lead instructors hold a summer orientation session for enrolling students to review expectations (e.g., workloads and the need for support from other students and family members) and some of the planned activities. Students receive the attendance policy, review first-day success tips, and preview textbooks.

Initial data demonstrated that TLC students were more successful in their English and psychology courses when compared with non-TLC students in the same courses. Although not a stated goal of the program, persistence was higher for the TLC students fall to fall compared with GTCC's overall fall-to-fall persistence rate for former developmental students. Because of budget limitations, however, GTCC continued to offer only one TLC each term, although the number of interested and eligible students increased.

Learning communities, with lower class sizes and reassigned time for instructors to develop them, increases costs well above the more traditional methods. However, students in the TLC were, in fact, more successful. An unintended benefit of this initiative was the gain in persistence of these students, leading to a higher probability of completion (graduation) than qualifying students who do not participate in the program. Stakeholders should recognize that this type of initiative should be considered a long-term investment that requires high initial costs. GTCC's learning communities are now centered on either developmental or transitional courses (GTCC, 2010).

Front-Door Center

Multiple services that first-year students may require are consolidated in one convenient area, including all intake services such as admissions, records, financial aid, placement testing, disability services, orientation, and counseling. Students are welcomed to this renovated area, where this front-door experience makes the intimidating enrollment process less so. Of the characteristics of successful developmental education courses and programs identified in numerous studies, GTCC has touched upon them all—including "becoming a more humane institution," with initiatives in place to make students feel welcome and get off on the right foot conveniently and with accurate information and that provide supplemental support services throughout the first semester in all courses. A holistic system of support, instruction, interventions, and administrative procedures to streamline and provide the best information works for the novice student, beginning with the front-door experience to the improved, mandatory orientation—a major success outcome of the ATD initiatives.

All first-time students enrolling at any community college need to get their feet on the ground in this new arena about which they may know little or nothing. All colleges provide orientation for faculty, even for those very experienced faculty who have taught in community colleges previous to their joining their current college family. As faculty and staff, we orient ourselves to new technology and systems that are important to navigate and implement teaching and learning pathways successfully. By the same token, those are, understandably and intuitively, critical steps toward student success in this unfamiliar territory. Beginning with the online options for completing the mandatory orientation, the college provides the critical flexibility for students whose schedules could not accommodate their being on site.

CONTINUING TO "CAUSE QUALITY"

Along with instructional interventions, increased student support systems, and revised administrative procedures, the developmental initiatives are firmly rooted in the strengths of holistic systems that embrace as full a range of services for the students most in need of them as possible. For example, 1-hour supplemental instruction sessions attached to some introductory algebra courses became mandatory. As was frequently reported in successful completion data, students "do not do optional." When data indicated that there were significantly promising trends in course completion and persistence in follow-up courses when the courses were required, they were made mandatory.

In conjunction with its data warehouse, GTCC accessed other measurement devices and strategies to learn more about its students and track the performance of the institution as a whole. Conducting surveys, such as CCSSE, the college could more readily access more data points and identify students' connections to and participation in college programs and services. Moreover, the college maintains a strong link to a broad network of colleges pursuing the same data collection strategies and collecting outcome data that, in addition to being shared with other CCCSE-member colleges, help forecast and identify promising trends and practices that have been the result of institutionally designed and initiated work. As these data-informed efforts continue, the concepts are reinforced that teaching and learning, educational attainment, and college completion should and do matter to and for everyone.

In spring 2009, GTCC applied to the Bill & Melinda Gates Foundation for a DEI grant, in the interest of expanding academic support services for students and substantially improving all educational experiences for developmental students. Excited about continuing and expanding the lessons learned in the 5 years of work initiated and implemented within the timeframe of the ATD grant, GTCC observed that the overarching goal of the DEI grant was to continue road-testing programs and strategies and initiatives representing the greatest promise for increasing the likelihood that students beginning their college experience with remedial course work would be able to complete their selected programs of study. Leveling the playing field was a critical outcome of ongoing program designs, initiatives, and strategies. In a 2009 letter of support for the grant application, the GTCC board chair stated, "The College is ready now to pull together a comprehensive, student-focused set of interventions that can be tailored to match students' unique needs and expanded to include all our development students" (S. Frye, personal communication, April 1, 2009).

The year-long grant was awarded, and GTCC began its work toward realizing this overarching goal—taking its successful interventions, begun during the ATD years, and expanding them across the college. GTCC's (2010) end-of-grant report recorded some remarkably successful efforts, among them the Advocacy Initiative. This initiative grew out of Tinto's 1994 study documenting improved persistence and success when students feel connected to the college. GTCC involved a range of college employees to serve as advocates for developmental students, who would meet with students throughout the semester to answer their questions and assist them with locating resources to help them overcome traditional barriers to attendance and success.

GTCC also reported some disappointments. However, the disappointments were conversationally described as learning opportunities for making modifications— especially to initiatives that suffered from timeline pressures, lack of data production software, key developmental personnel changes, and dramatic enrollment increases that resulted in additional faculty hires with resulting impact on communication and professional development.

Modifications were made to all initiatives, and no initiatives were to be discontinued. The work to tweak the initiatives would continue, based on experiences that captured some continuing promise. The DEI grant provided the relative luxury of more road-test time, allowing for modifications that are still being made. Challenges continue, as they do in all colleges, but articulating them has helped GTCC focus on its "soft spots," which GTCC identified as follows:

- Minority students, male students, and students under 26 years of age are less successful than many of their counterparts.
- GTCC is growing so fast that bringing programs up to scale will be difficult in the current economy.
- The need for developmental education is rising, and these students are most at risk for dropping out of college.
- New issues facing students will arise that will require additional effective interventions. (Center for Applied Research, 2009)

Highs and Lows

ATD honored GTCC with the 2010 Leah Meyer Austin Institutional Student Success Leadership Award. The award was created by the Lumina Foundation in honor of its former senior vice president for program development and organizational learning, who helped shape the development of the national ATD initiative to improve student success in community colleges. The award announcement stated: "How GTCC, which earned Achieving the Dream Leader College status in 2009, built a culture of evidence to achieve equity and excellence is a lesson in the power of high-level commitment and well-focused grassroots action" (ATD, 2010).

It has taken community colleges a long time to get to this place, relative to student success, in which they find themselves challenged by the numbers of students who pass through their doors and then so frequently exit without having achieved their academic goals. Access has for so long been at the heart of the community college mission, and it has been an extraordinarily successful mission. However, increasing public concern and demand require that colleges do better and advance success as the more dominant, overarching mission. Open access does, indeed, make community colleges unique in the world of higher education. However, in the scheme of the student experience, success matters more. As Shelly (2011) observed: "College admissions dramas make for good reading. Jobs and financial security make for happier endings" (p. A9).

GTCC embraced, promoted, and supported open discussion about experiments, trial runs, innovative attempts to change student outcomes, on all levels, but especially for those students who were at greatest academic risk. It did so knowing that all discussions relative to particular student populations (e.g., specific to developmental levels, gender, ethnicity, and age) and to the data about student retention and completion would be "risky" endeavors (Zachry & Orr, 2009, p. 52). For example, GTCC, along with many others operating in areas where competition can be fierce for student dollars and bodies, recognized the need to be candid about the realities associated with student experiences and to articulate clearly the strategies that the college is employing to make student experiences productive and valuable. However, simultaneously, it understood that some caution was required in communicating with its communities about outcome data.

After 5 years as an ATD college and working hard along with others struggling to address similar issues in their own colleges hard at work in the ATD initiative, GTCC was disappointed in the apparently small and rarely measurable differences in student performance and achievement. All along, there were cautionary reminders to members of the college family most involved with the ATD work, at all levels, to stay the course and embrace the realization that change on so many fronts would be difficult, but not impossible tasks. There were reasons (and data) to suggest, at the end of the 5-year ATD experience and well into the DEI experience, that pockets of success with great promise had proven to be worthy of further implementation, tweaking, time, and study. Some successes would be undercut or rendered impossible by cost and, ultimately, could not be taken to scale. Others would require more time to discern if they were flashes in the pan or would remain as legitimate successes across time and student populations, and the like.

But with all of that, GTCC had to determine its best course for communicating the multiple perceptions of the reality within which it was living, and keep the community engaged and supportive and accepting of its efforts. Understandably, a major recommendation made in Zachry and Orr's 2009 report, under "Lessons for the Initiative from Guilford's Experience," focused on helping colleges get a handle on how best to tell their stories to stakeholders. The researchers saw the need to "help colleges consider the most appropriate methods for evaluating student success, and provide recommendations for colleges about how to share their data with external audiences" (p. 52).

In *Pitch Perfect: Communicating with Traditional and Social Media for Scholars, Researchers, and Academic Leaders*, media consultant William Tyson (2010) advised to above all "tell the truth, tell the truth, tell the truth." Tell that truth in a story that will capture the attention of a wider audience—outside of your own institution or organization or otherwise compartmentalized ideas, help educate that audience about the value of the message, and make it relevant to their interests. Tyson further noted that frequently when individuals and institutions in the academic arena move to advise the general public about sensitive quality and access issues, they often are hesitant to work with mainstream media to tell their stories, that they translate marketing and public relations as spin that is intended to distort or create a bias about the real issues. The bottom line is to share what you know and to be willing to invest time in developing relationships that generate conversations. Tyson (2011) asserted that "conversations are more productive than news releases" and more likely to generate the public relations that serve the institution's best interests.

Moreover, while GTCC recognized that the work would be difficult and slow, it had also committed itself to some ambitious goals and done so in very precarious economic times. It needed to take these realities in stride and fold them into the story that would be told to its communities. The backdrop and the context would be critical components of the full story about change, time, and perseverance. Wrapping itself around the story and bringing it to life is GTCC's task—to explain the disappointments and the promises to the internal and external audiences upon which the college depends for its support and to help them all better embrace the full measure of the enormous challenge and the remarkable potential associated with stepping up with outcome data to address them.

LESSONS LEARNED

- Interest in student success must begin at the highest levels and be sustained by genuine, proactive, unwavering attention to the details of student and institutional performance. Perception is reality. When individuals across the college perceive and believe that leadership is squarely in their corner, they trust their instincts. Student success is the outcome that must be measured and matter in college policy, in academic programming, and in community support.
- There must be an abiding, affirming, shared belief in the power of "courageous conversations" about student achievements, even when they can frequently put the institution simultaneously in the driver's seat and the hot seat. The public's patience is short, and confidence is easily shaken or lost, especially if change—even if well-intended and purpose-driven—is perceived as without value, too costly, or too slow. Staying the course, collecting meaningful data, and engaging the larger audience in the college's story can make the story about its works in progress more palatable, transparent, and believable.
- A systematic, planned program for student engagement, one that gets students involved with the college in a meaningful way, must be an institutional priority. One way to do this is by providing advocates to keep communication lines open and students in touch with the human side of the academic enterprise. Students, staff, faculty, and counselors can serve as advocates for both targeted and general-population students, all in the interest of keeping students connected psychologically and physically. Collecting data that address the outcomes of an advocacy program might well provide the support necessary for arguing the logic of continued funding that ultimately will generate the FTE to sustain an advocacy initiative. Moreover, learning communities have been identified as promising strategies for strengthening student-to-student and student-to-instructor relationships.
- Colleges should introduce students to college by ensuring a smooth and organized enrollment process and by supplying sufficient information at the front door.
- A one-size-fits-all approach will not work to improve student achievements at all levels and for all populations, nor are there many clear paths to identifying approaches that will work. Common-sense strategies often are

the answers to common-sense questions. As aggravatingly slow as they may be, trial-and-error road tests continue to be the most solid approaches to determining whether or not the sense is so common, after all. In a one-size-fits-all system, students' individual needs will fall through the academic and institutional cracks. Targeted success strategies may work best, and individualized case management and advocacy models for admission, placement testing, advising, and registration hold promise.

- Student orientation that provides accurate information, assessment, and enrollment guidance must be mandatory.
- Collecting feedback from students is essential to a college's decision making about programs and initiatives. Formal and informal surveys and focus groups are valuable sources of information about how well initiatives are working. Student representatives could provide important information to college personnel by serving on college committees charged with responsibility for institutional effectiveness and student success.
- Specific benchmarks for institutional performance should be established and discussed across the college. Whether implemented via an institutional scorecard or by other regular reports about the results of data collection and analysis, colleges should track progress systematically, using indicators such as rates of graduation, persistence, engagement, and developmental achievement. Teams or committees that are designed to engage all college personnel help disseminate important information across campus and bring diverse talents and ideas to the table.
- Data collection and analysis is best conducted when all faculty and staff are involved in the activity and in the implementation of changes based on the results. The more common concerns expressed by faculty and staff when they are approached to conduct research and analyze data are lack of time and doubts that performance can be measurably affected by improving individual classroom practices.
- Colleges must attend to meeting the needs of the communities they serve. Meeting those needs in the short and long run is hard work, because the needs are as diverse as the individual students' needs. Attending to student success is key to a community's trust.

REFERENCES

Achieving the Dream. (2010, February). *Achieving the Dream honors Guilford Technical Community College.* Available from http://www.aacc.nche.edu/About/completionchallenge/Documents/2010AustinAwardBrochure.pdf

American Association of Community Colleges. (2012). *About VFA.* Available from http://www.aacc.nche.edu/Resources/aaccprograms/VFAWeb/Pages/AboutVFA.aspx

American Association of Community Colleges, the Association of Community College Trustees, the Center for Community College Student Engagement, the League for Innovation in the Community College, the National Institute for Staff and Organizational Development, and Phi Theta Kappa. (2010, April). *Democracy's colleges: Call to action.* Washington, DC: American Association of Community Colleges. Available from http://www.aacc.nche.edu/About/completionchallenge/Documents/calltoaction.pdf

Bailey, T. (2009). Challenge and opportunity: Rethinking the role and function of developmental education in community colleges. *New directions for community colleges, 145,* pp. 11–30.

Bailey, T., & Cho, S. (2010, October). *Developmental education in community colleges* [Issue brief]. New York, NY: Columbia University, Teachers College, Community College Research Center. Available from http://ccrc.tc.columbia.edu/Publication.asp?UID=815

Bailey, T., Jeong, D.W., & Cho, S. (2010). Referral, enrollment, and completion in developmental education sequences in community colleges. *Economics of Education Review, 29*(2), 255–270.

Bill & Melinda Gates Foundation. (2008, December 9). *New initiative to double the number of low-income students in the U.S. who earn a postsecondary degree by age 26* [Press release]. Available from http://www.gatesfoundation.org/press-releases/Pages/low-income-postsecondary-degree-081209.aspx

Boylan, H. R. (2002). *What works: Research-based practices in developmental education.* Boone, NC: National Center for Developmental Education.

Center for Applied Research. (2009). *Five-year summative evaluation of the Achieving the Dream initiative for Guilford Technical Community College.* Charlotte, NC: Central Piedmont Community College.

Center for Community College Student Engagement. (2010). *The heart of student success: Teaching, learning, and college completion.* Austin, TX: Author.

Center for Community College Student Engagement. (2012). *A matter of degrees: Promising practices for community college student success.* Austin, TX: Author.

College Board. (2011). *Trends in college pricing 2011.* Available from http://trends.collegeboard.org/downloads/College_Pricing_2011.pdf

Ewell, P. T. (2006). *Making the grade: How boards can ensure academic quality.* Washington, DC: Association of Governing Boards and Universities and Colleges.

Guilford Technical Community College. (2010, April 30). *Annual report.*

Guilford Technical Community College. (2011, July 18). *Mentoring provides insights for students in GTCC program* [News release]. Available from http://www.gtcc.edu/news/mentoring-provides-insights-for-students-in-gtcc-program.aspx

Katsinas, S. G., D'Amico, M. M., & Friedel, J. N. (2011, September 15). *Access and funding in public higher education—the 2011 national survey.* Tuscaloosa, AL: Education Policy Center.

Larose, G. [n.d.]. Student retention at community colleges: Engaging a new generation with technology is key to America's future [White paper]. Available from http://www.webstudy.com/download/WebStudy_Whitepaper.pdf

Lumina Foundation. (2012). *Goal 2025*. Available from http://www.luminafoundation.org/goal_2025.html

Marklein, M. (2008, November). Report: Community colleges must expect more. *USA Today*, pp. 11–16.

Massey, E. R., & Hart, C. T. (2010, Fall/Winter). Realizing potential: It's about the culture. *Community college entrepreneurship*, pp. 6–7, 26–27.

McClenney, B. (2010). *Top ten reasons for progress in Achieving the Dream.* Unpublished document.

Mullin, C. M. (2010, September). *Doing more with less: The inequitable funding of community colleges* [Policy brief]. Washington, DC: American Association of Community Colleges.

National Commission on Community Colleges. (2008, January). *Winning the skills race and strengthening America's middle class: An action agenda for community colleges.* New York, NY: The College Board.

National Commission on Excellence in Education. (1983, April). *A nation at risk: The imperative for educational reform.* Washington, DC: U.S. Department of Education.

O'Banion, T. (2010, October/November). The completion agenda: To what end? *Community College Journal*, pp. 44–47.

Rutschow, E. Z., Richburg-Hayes, L., Brock, T., Orr, G., Cerna, O., Cullinan, D., Kerrigan, M. R., Jenkins, D., Gooden, S., & Martin, K. (2011). *Turning the tide: Five years of Achieving the Dream in community colleges.* New York, NY: MDRC. Available from http://www.mdrc.org/publications/578/full.pdf

Seymour, D. (1993). *On Q: Causing quality in higher education.* Phoenix, AZ: American Council on Education and The Oryx Press.

Shelly, B. (2011, April 20). Opinion. *Austin American-Statesman*, A9.

Tinto, V. (1994). *Leaving college: Rethinking the causes and cures of student attrition* (2nd ed.). Chicago: University of Chicago Press.

Tinto, V. (1998). *Learning communities and the reconstruction of remedial education in higher education.* Presentation at the Conference on Replacing Remediation in Higher Education, Stanford University, January 26–29.

Tyson, W. (2010). *Pitch perfect: Communicating with traditional and social media for scholars, researchers, and academic leaders.* Sterling, VA: Stylus Publishing.

Tyson, W. (2011, January 21). Scholar as public intellectual. *Inside Higher Ed.*

White House. (2009, July 14). *Remarks by the president on the American Graduation Initiative.* Available from http://www.whitehouse.gov/the_press_office/Remarks-by-the-President-on-the-American-Graduation-Initiative-in-Warren-MI

Zachry, E. M., & Orr, G. (2009, September). *Building student success from the ground up: A case study of an Achieving the Dream college.* New York, NY: MDRC. Available from http://www.mdrc.org/publications/526/overview.html

SUGGESTED READING

Roueche, J. E., Ely, E. E., & Roueche, S. D. (2001). *In pursuit of excellence: The Community College of Denver.* Washington, DC: Community College Press.

Roueche, J. E., & Roueche, S. D. (1993). *Between a rock and a hard place: The at-risk student in the open-door college.* Washington, DC: Community College Press.

Roueche, J. E., & Roueche, S. D. (1999). *High stakes, high performance: Making remedial education work.* Washington, DC: Community College Press.

CHAPTER 4

Establishing Relationships for a Healthy P–16 Pipeline

Melinda M. Valdez-Ellis

The Challenge:

Large numbers of students come to college unprepared for college-level work.

The Response:

Building relationships with the entire education community to ensure that students receive the preparation they need all through the education pipeline.

If people begin to see the educational system as a single entity through which people move, they may begin to behave as if all of education were related. The time has come to implement change with the emergence of P-16.

— H. L. Hodgkinson (1985)

A ll education leaders strive to facilitate student achievement growth, especially for children from families of lower socioeconomic status. To this end, educators, policymakers, and others, including states and local communities, have investigated concepts and methods to create an enhanced approach to education in which all levels of education—preschool through college—coordinate, communicate, and educate as one integrated system. In this regard, there has been a growing awareness that the educational process begins at birth and extends from prekindergarten through high school and to postsecondary education and beyond. Collectively, these initiatives and efforts have become known as the P–16 concept of education—the letter *P* representing preschool and the number *16* representing attainment of a bachelor's degree.

RECOGNIZING STUDENTS' NEEDS THROUGHOUT THE PIPELINE

The socioeconomic status (SES) of students' families is a key factor for educators to consider when assessing learning outcomes. Research indicates that only 65% of students from lower SES earn a high school diploma, compared with 91% of students from the middle and upper levels (Hoffman, Vargas, Venezia, & Miller, 2007). In the past decade, North Carolina has been ranked as one of the top 10 states with the highest high school dropout rate (Cataldi, Laird, & KewalRamani, 2009).

As expected, the lack of adequate academic preparation leads to high college failure rates. While 1 out of every 2 students from middle- and upper-class families can be expected to earn a college degree, only 1 in 10 students from the lowest SES group will do so (Steinberg & Almeida, 2008). A decade of research has demonstrated that low-income and minority students can achieve at exceptionally high rates when provided with the high expectations, reasonable resources, and ample opportunities.

that are commonplace in our nation's best schools. Armed with these facts, at Guilford Technical Community College (GTCC), Donald Cameron facilitated and championed opportunities for the continued, future success of students who were traditionally "lost" in the education pipeline between high school and postsecondary education.

High School to Postsecondary Education

There is a significant gap between what high school teachers and students think is needed for earning a high school diploma and what college professors and employers say is required for success in college and the workplace. Positive efforts to help ease the transition from high school to college include making high school curriculum academically rigorous and improving communication and outreach between postsecondary institutions and high schools. In order to link these two distinct educational entities, an economic imperative might be to explore P–16 programs, as noted by the National Commission on the High School Senior Year:

> As the knowledge and skill demands of the new economy have increased, there is increasing consensus among economists (and among families) that virtually all young people need the knowledge and skills necessary to benefit from postsecondary education—both on the job and in formal postsecondary institutions. In short, whether a student progresses from postsecondary education to a job, or to a first job which ultimately leads to enrollment in postsecondary education, *all* students need high-level academic knowledge and skills associated with college preparatory studies. (cited in Somerville & Yi, 2002, p. 28)

P–16 programs provide a powerful framework to improve teaching and learning and, thus, better prepare students for living, learning, and working in a changing world. The major ideas surrounding P–16 efforts include the desire to align school districts with higher education. The primary goal is an integrated system of education that encourages student achievement; results in more students progressing to postsecondary education; and produces better outcomes for students, educators, and communities (Rochford, O'Neill, Gelb, & Ross, 2005). The National Skills Coalition (2010) estimated that by 2014, 80% of the jobs available in North Carolina will require some amount of college or training beyond high school.

This is not a new concept to most educational leaders who understand that jobs in today's workforce require more education and training than were required just 30 years ago. A Brookings Institution brief, *The Future of Middle-Skill Jobs* (Holzer & Lerman, 2009), revealed that the middle-skill employment share in North Carolina for 2006 was almost 25% higher than that of high-skill jobs, and it was higher than the national average. Table 4.1 shows the middle-skill occupations requiring postsecondary training or an associate degree that are projected to grow the fastest from 2008 to 2016.

GTCC provides a variety of options for postsecondary success through specific, innovative programs aligned with the goals of P–16. These options include training for some of the highest median-income occupations that also are among the fastest-growing occupations in North Carolina (e.g., dental hygienist). GTCC has explored additional occupations that are among the fastest growing but selects those with the most promising income potential as good options for the curriculum.

Table 4.1: Fastest-Growing Middle-Skill Occupations in North Carolina: 2008–2016				
Occupation	Employment			Median Income
	2008	2018	% change	
Dental hygienists	5,180	7,350	+42%	$62,800
Veterinary technologists and technicians	2,360	3,330	+41%	$26,100
Medical equipment repairers	530	710	+35%	$46,700
Surgical technologists	3,050	4,050	+33%	$37,600
Skin care specialists	1,150	1,490	+30%	$33,800
Cardiovascular technologists and technicians	1,240	1,610	+30%	$57,400

Note. Middle-skill occupations are defined in the data sort as those requiring postsecondary training or an associate degree. From U.S. Department of Labor (2011).

P–16 Progress at the Community College Level

Community colleges historically have served as institutions accessible by anyone wishing to enter through their doors. In his seminal book, *The Community College: Values, Vision, and Vitality,* former president of the American Association of Community Colleges Edmund Gleazer (2000) described the driving forces of the mission of community colleges as adaptability, sustaining relationships with students, and community focus. The ability of a community college to adapt to the changing needs of its community and maintain sustainable relationships with students is at the core of collaboration between community colleges and public high schools.

According to a special report in *The Chronicle of Higher Education* (Haycock, 2006), 60 of every 100 ninth-grade students in this country do not enroll in college immediately after graduating high school, and only 50% of those students who attend college pursue a college-preparatory curriculum while in high school. In addition to saving time and money, allowing underrepresented students to move through high school to postsecondary education more quickly than they would traditionally increases their motivation to do so. Collaboration simultaneously improves the college utilization rate and reduces the overall cost of an individual student's educational experiences.

Successful collaborative initiatives between higher education and K–12 efforts are commanding the attention of policymakers and educational leaders at the community, state, and national levels. Increasing the educational attainment of our population is essential to advancing our nation's efforts for academic excellence. The following are three examples of effective initiatives.

- Stephen Portch, chancellor emeritus of the University System of Georgia, who instituted the first local and regional P–16s in 1995, has called the Stark Education Partnership (Stark County, OH) the finest local P–16 in the nation. In 1989, Stark was Ohio's first local P–16; now 22 such councils exist in the state (see Stark Education Partnership, 2009, 2010). The partnership promotes early college high schools and dual-credit programs with community colleges in the state.
- Washington State's Running Start Program was created in 1990, as part of the Learning by Choice law that allows 11th- and 12th-grade students to take courses at the state's 34 technical and community colleges (and participating state universities). The program and legislation are models that have been replicated in other states, including Oregon and Minnesota (see Brand & Lerner, 2006).
- The El Paso Collaborative for Academic Excellence is in its 20th year, as it strives to align policies at the secondary and postsecondary levels. El Paso Community College (TX) and the University of Texas at El Paso eliminated remedial classes for students, and high schools increased graduation standards to require 4 years of math and science in order to graduate (see El Paso Collaborative for Academic Excellence, 2010). Instead of taking remedial classes, high school students are offered extra assistance in these courses.

P–16 INITIATIVES AT GTCC

The limited impact of traditional educational programs to serve the needs and potential success of high school students prompted Cameron to develop programs better attuned to the life situations of students in the community. Cognizant of the potential of the P–16 concept to provide a seamless system of education for GTCC students, Cameron embraced several nontraditional methods involving collaboration with the third-largest school district in North Carolina, Guilford County Schools (GCS). These include middle colleges and early middle colleges, college tech prep, and the Area School Assistance Program.

An educational collaboration between a high school and a college requires that these two traditionally closed institutions of education analyze the assumptions that had allowed each to exist as if the other did not. It demands financial, administrative, and programmatic support. Cameron presented a dedicated, visionary plea to all stakeholders, moved forward, and persisted in making it a reality. GTCC's mission includes offering outreach programs geared toward high school students and, thus, announces the accessibility of its higher education services to all.

Two common goals of P–16 involve high school and higher education. One creates a wider range of learning experiences and opportunities for students in high school, especially in the final 2 years. The other improves college readiness and success. Middle colleges seek to meet these two goals by affording high school students the opportunity to earn a high school diploma and transferable college credits upon graduation. When Terry Grier arrived as the new Guilford County Schools (GSC) superintendent in 2000, he sought to enhance GSC–GTCC partnership capabilities by presenting the middle college concept to GTCC's president at the time, Donald Cameron. The partnership seeks to enrich academically capable students who are on the path to dropping out of high school by offering them an alternative academic environment.

Middle colleges have been in operation since 1974. Beginning in 2002, with funding from the Bill & Melinda Gates Foundation, many middle colleges became new or redesigned early colleges, allowing students opportunities to earn up to 2 full years of transferable college credit or an associate degree. One of the most significant enhancements to the postsecondary services provided to GCS and GTCC students occurred with the first middle college in 2001. Again, as with countless other partnership opportunities, Cameron's enthusiasm for partnerships reinforced Grier's plans to bring the middle college concept to fruition.

School administrators lined up to chronicle the obstacles of generating buy-in for new programs among board members, faculty, staff, students, and the community. Even as the student success goal is presumably shared by all educators, innovative ideas to increase student engagement are often met with resistance, perhaps driven by an inherent fear of change. Cameron worked to introduce the middle college concept to stakeholders. He was able to convey this vision and this idea at many formal and informal meetings, eventually leading the boards of both educational institutions to embrace change with the acceptance of the Early/Middle College at GTCC–Jamestown.

Early/Middle College at GTCC–Jamestown

An early/middle college opened at GTCC's Jamestown campus in 2001 as North Carolina's first middle college high school, specifically designed for high school juniors and seniors who were at risk of not graduating in the traditional high school setting. The school's mission was to have a 100% graduation rate for a diverse student body, with a rigorous and relevant curriculum, supported by a positive faculty.

In 2005, the college accepted its first cohort of first-year high school students, allowing these students to begin their path in the early college strand to ensure they graduated with both a high school diploma and an associate degree or 2 years of college credit. In turn, it continued to allow junior and senior middle college students to enroll in college courses for dual high school and college credit without the requirement of obtaining an associate degree upon high school graduation.

The students attend classes from 11:00 a.m. until 4:45 p.m. daily, following GTCC's academic-year calendar. The complete program emphasizes academic preparation and incorporates career exploration into the curriculum to ensure that students experience relevance for the development of the total individual. It offers a diverse academic curriculum, including honors courses in English, mathematics, science, foreign languages, and social studies. Students enjoy access to all GTCC resources, including the library, cafeteria, and computer labs.

After one decade, the Early/Middle College GTCC–Jamestown had earned recognition and several awards, including

- North Carolina Lighthouse Schools Award (2002)
- One of 10 Most Improved High Schools in North Carolina (2003)
- One of five accelerated "Learn and Earn" model high schools named by North Carolina Governor Easley (2004)
- Signature School Award (2005)
- Celebration of Excellence Most Improved School Award (2005)

Principal Loretta Rowland-Kitley observed:

We make sure we keep in contact with our students during the summer to continue the progression of our relationships. They know we will go the extra mile for them, so they do the same in return. Our focus is on progress … [we are] not expecting each student to have a perfect GPA each year. They feel safe in our school because the teachers and administration are completely focused on them—that is key. (personal communications, August 17, 2010)

Early/Middle College at GTCC–Greensboro

This early/middle college opened its doors in 2005. Special project simulations and seminars to help students integrate academic experience with academic goals are offered to all students. The class of 2009 consisted of 126 students in grades 9–12, evenly balanced by gender. The composition of the class by race/ethnicity was as follows: Black, 54%; White, 33%; multiracial, 7%; Hispanic, 3%; Asian American, 2%; and Native American, 1%. All teaching staff held credentials in their disciplines—60% had master's, specialty, or doctoral degrees; 20% were certified by the National Board for Professional Teaching Standards (Guilford County School District, 2010).

All of the members of the class of 2009 planned to attend a postsecondary institution—52% planned to attend a 4-year college or university and 48% to attend a 2-year college or technical school. Nearly half completed the college/university prep course of study—24% completed the college technical prep course of study, and 24% completed both programs of study (Guilford County School District, 2010).

Beginning with the class of 2010, all students are required to complete the college/university prep course of study. Students may be eligible to begin taking college courses through GTCC as early as their sophomore year of high school. Students are required to participate in at least one noncredit seminar course each semester. Noncredit seminar course topics include tutorials, time management, study skills, test-taking strategies, decision-making, goal setting, and college/career planning.

Early/Middle College at GTCC–High Point

The early/middle college at GTCC's High Point campus launched its programs in 2006. Its mission is to guide students toward higher education while preparing them to be lifelong learners and productive members of society. This goal is pursued by employing personalized and engaging instruction, establishing a nurturing team environment, and focusing on rigor, relevance, and relationships. The school serves 125 students each year, with a staff of 15 and a maximum class size of 17 students per class. As with all of the middle colleges at GTCC, GCS pays for all textbooks and tuition for college-level courses.

Students interested in attending the college are provided with the opportunity to explore music industry classes, as the High Point campus is the home of the Larry Gatlin School of Entertainment Technology. Middle-college students have the option of enrolling in other general college courses offered by GTCC, as well as elective courses, which include television broadcasting and production and scientific visualizations.

***

A key factor in sustaining the early/middle college programs is GTCC's early/middle college program liaison, who manages the operational needs of the schools and maintains open communication among the school administrators and school faculty and staff members to ensure that student success goals are the priority of both educational institutions. Creating a relationship with the superintendent has enabled ongoing communication between high school and GTCC chief administrators, faculty, and counselors. All parties involved share common concerns about student success and educational continuity.

COLLEGE TECH PREP PROGRAM

Viewed as one of the most innovative and effective educational reform efforts in American history, college tech prep is a workforce program that connects learning to career pathways and teaches students the knowledge, skills, and behaviors they need to compete successfully in the high-tech workplace (Hull & Grevelle, 1998). The workforce program provides each student with

- A career pathway with an identified sequence of courses that enhances technological skills and employability.
- Advanced occupational training identified in partnership with business and industry.
- Articulated programs leading to certificate or degree.
- A curriculum integrating academic and occupational learning and application.

In 1993, Guilford County merged its three public schools into one system that became GCS. Before this merger, it was difficult to facilitate agreements between the three individual school systems. There were many unsuccessful attempts in the 1980s to put tech prep on the dashboard of any school system in the county. Shortly after the merger in 1993, business and industry leaders began to meet with the first GCS superintendent, Jerry Weast (served 1993–2000), to discuss the lack of technically prepared young adults in the area.

By the early 1990s, Cameron had long desired to create a plan that would address the needs of the changing economy while also involving GCS and community leadership from the business and industry sectors. During that time, he had developed a firm grasp of the unfavorable impression that GTCC was not producing highly skilled graduates for local business and industry. This community perception served as an additional catalyst for Cameron to pursue a workforce partnership after failed attempts to do so with the previous three unwilling pre-merger school superintendents.

Almost simultaneously, as would happen almost a full decade later with the middle college proposal, Cameron utilized his skills of relationship-building with the new superintendent to pursue one of the most comprehensive workforce preparedness assessments ever achieved in the county. Together, Cameron and Weast worked with their teams and area business leaders to respond to the assessment's recommendations. As a result of listening to more than 700 county citizens in focus group discussions and telephone interviews, a comprehensive program for GCS was implemented in the 1993–1994 school year, which provided

- A career-awareness curriculum and instruction plan in elementary schools.
- A career-exploration program in middle schools.
- A career-preparation focus in high schools.

Cameron was aware that introducing a new plan is best communicated in multiple venues. He utilized a series of seminars, luncheons, and workshops to acquaint all stakeholders with the new concept. All incoming ninth graders received an explanation detailing the program's advantages and expected outcomes. High school students were assisted with course decisions via a tech prep curriculum manual, adopted later as a model by the North Carolina Community College System.

GCS initiated courses of study that vertically aligned with GTCC's 2-year technical degrees, thereby creating nine college tech prep courses aligned to GTCC's associate in applied sciences programs. Over 375 four-course sequences are available to GCS high school students as they aspire for tech prep completer status in one of the 10 courses of study. The College Tech Prep Program at GTCC is a seamless education program that embodies P–16 goals as it connects elementary school students to higher education. Students earn an associate degree, a 2-year certificate, or a 2-year registered apprenticeship upon completion of the program.

Judging by the recognition it has received over the years, the College Tech Program at GTCC can be considered one of the most successful in North Carolina (see Table 4.2). The partnership received national recognition in 1999 from the American School Board Association and the American Association of Community Colleges. The program also triggered the creation of the Youth Apprenticeship Program, beginning with 23 students working for six area companies. In addition, the Cooperative

Table 4.2: Recognition for GTCC's College Tech Prep Program	
Date	**Recognition**
2004–2007	Promotion of College Tech Prep Award, Partnership Excellence Award, and Overall Program Excellence Award —For outstanding accomplishment
2003/2004	Governor's Education First Partnership Award —For collaborative effort to bring the first Red Hat Acadamy and develop a strong IT program for Guilford County Schools.
2002	Governor's Business Partnership Award —For impact of expertise, volunteer, in-kind, and financial support to public education.
2000/2001	Outstanding High School Apprentice Program (Guilford County College Tech Prep Automotive Council and Construction Council)
2000	—With funding from the National School-to-Work Office, the Center for Occupational Research and Development (CORD) conducted a study of effective programs that strongly support the transition of students into higher education and the workplace. GTCC's College Tech Prep program was one of 11 secondary and postsecondary partnerships cited in its final report (Walde, 2000). GTCC's program was chosen as an exemplar because it provides the structured linkages between secondary and postsecondary education inherent in tech prep.
1999	R.J. Reynolds Outstanding Overall College Tech Prep Reform Effort Award
1998	R.J. Reynolds Outstanding College Tech Prep Marketing
1997	R.J. Reynolds Outstanding College Tech Prep Collaboration and Partnership

Education Program offers students the chance to unite academic study with practical on-the-job experience through 32 courses of study, allowing students to work with 57 employers.

Since the late 1990s, a scholarship program launched by Cameron has provided the cost of 2 years of tuition and fees to college tech prep completers who enrolled in 2-year associate in applied science programs at GTCC, allowing them to continue their technical training from high school. In its first year, 10 tech prep scholarships were awarded; 3 years later, a total of 85 scholarships had been awarded. In the past decade, more than 2,000 students have attended GTCC in the scholarship program, receiving $150,000–$200,000 in total scholarship awards.

AREA SCHOOL ASSISTANCE PROGRAM

Until the early 1980s the three local school boards in the county were reluctant to endorse the idea of a partnership with GTCC. When GTCC began to offer transfer options of general education credits to 4-year institutions, the county's private universities increased their marketing efforts to gain leverage with potential students. In 1983, Cameron, who was then vice president for instruction at the college, led a team to begin the Area School Assistance Program (ASAP).

At least one guidance counselor or career development coordinator from each GCS high school is hired during the summer to facilitate ASAP initiatives. These hires participate in an orientation session that explains program goals and contacts graduating seniors to discuss their plans for college and offer information about GTCC programs. Once students are identified as not having concrete postsecondary plans, GTCC attempts to recruit and enroll them in the upcoming fall semester. Admissions advisor Mike Mackey explained the program's goals as follows:

> We want to communicate with those students who haven't indicated their plans after graduating from high school. We inform them of the opportunities here at GTCC. The counselors are able to do this for the students after meeting with our employees from admissions, financial aid, and student life during their ASAP orientation.

On average, approximately 20% of graduating GCS high school seniors identified themselves as undecided for their postsecondary education plans. As a result, of the approximately 1,200–1,500 graduating seniors who are referred to GTCC by an ASAP coordinator, 300 to 550 students enroll in GTCC within the next academic year following their high school graduation (personal communication, M. Mackey, August 17, 2010).

The program was designed to give local high school students a review of GTCC programs and admission policies. In addition to the increased marketing and recruiting benefits, GTCC benefits from the program—the relationship forged with the local schools is the highlight of this successful venture. The program benefits public schools in the area and GTCC. Cameron expressed the value of the program: "The program built a high school counselor family of ambassadors for GTCC, and it also put the college on a path to change its weak relationship into a strong relationship with the public schools in the area" (personal communication, August 19, 2010).

———————•◦•———————

The higher education goals of P–16 have enjoyed a successful and progressive growth within the GTCC community. Realizing the importance of working together to overcome barriers such as incompatibility of curricula, inadequate information, and differences in educational philosophies, has been key to exposing students to the challenges of work and citizenship. Cameron understood that the results of these efforts are better-informed, better-prepared, and better-qualified high school and college students who enjoy an enhanced quality of life in their community as productive, contributing citizens. He found the link between educational attainment and economic development that continues to foster opportunities for learning success.

LESSONS LEARNED

- Advocate for P–16 success. Educate yourself, other leaders in all levels of education, and community members about the benefits and successes of a P–16 integrated education.
- Avoid long-standing attitudes suggesting a rivalry between K–12 and higher education. Ignoring this perception will promote improved chances of student success and thus better prepare students for living, learning, and working in a changing world. Welcome opportunities to collaborate.
- Invest your time and efforts in nontraditional methods of educational collaboration. Continue to support successful traditional methods of educational collaboration and be open to exploring other avenues for success (e.g., early college high schools—a concept extending beyond dual credit and concurrent enrollment, with many more elements to facilitate student success).
- Be a facilitator by allowing newly created or current programs to foster the development of new initiatives. The idea for the Youth Apprenticeship Program was ignited during the first college tech prep discussions between Cameron and Weast.

REFERENCES

Brand, B. & Lerner, J. B. (2006). *The college ladder: Linking secondary and postsecondary education success for all*. Retrieved from http://www.aypf.org/publications/The%20 College%20Ladder/TheCollegeLadderlinkingsecondaryandpostsecondaryeducation. pdf

Cataldi, E. F., Laird, J., & KewalRamani, A. (2009). *High school dropout and completion rates in the United States: 2007* (NCES 2009-064). U.S. Department of Education, Institute of Education Sciences, National Center for Education Statistics.

El Paso Collaboration for Academic Excellence. (2010). *Results*. Retrieved from http:// utminers.utep.edu/amartinez49/results.htm

Gleazer, E. J., Jr. (2000). *The community college: Values, vision and vitality*. Washington, DC: Community College Press.

Guilford County School District. (2010). *Early-middle college school at GTCC-Greensboro school profile*. Retrieved from http://www.gcsnc.com/education/ school/schoolhistory.php?sectiondetailid=189443&linkid=nav-menu-container-4-953841

Haycock, K. (2006, March 10). Student readiness: The challenge for colleges. *The Chronicle of Higher Education*.

Hodgkinson, H. L. (1985). *All one system*. Washington, DC: Institute for Educational Leadership.

Hoffman, N., Vargas, J., Venezia, A., & Miller, M. S. (2007). *Minding the gap: Why integrating high school with college makes sense and how to do it*. Cambridge, MA: Harvard Education Press.

Holzer, H. J., & Lerman, R. I. (2009). *The future of middle-skill jobs*. Retrieved from http://www.brookings.edu/papers/2009/02_middle_skill_jobs_holzer.aspx

Hull, D., & Grevelle, J. (1998). *Tech prep: The next generation*. Waco, TX: Center for Occupational Research and Development, Inc.

National Skills Coalition. (2010). *How prepared are North Carolina students for postsecondary success?* Retrieved from http://www.postsecconnect.org/files/ North%20Carolina.pdf

Rochford, J. A., O'Neill, A., Gelb, A., & Ross, K. J. (2005). *P–16: The last education reform*. Stark Education Partnership. Retrieved from http://www.eric.ed.gov/ ERICDocs/data/ericdocs2sql/content_storage_01/000019b/80/28/00/f8.pdf

Somerville, J., & Yi, Y. (2002). *Aligning K–12 and postsecondary expectations: State policy in transition*. Washington, DC: National Association of System Heads.

Stark Education Partnership. (2009). *Significant change*. Retrieved from http://www. edpartner.org/pdfs/significant_change.pdf

Stark Education Partnership. (2010). *Stark P–16 compact*. Retrieved from http://www. edpartner.org/initiatives/

Steinberg, A., & Almeida, C. A. (2008). *Raising graduation rates in an era of high standards*. Retrieved from http://www.achieve.org/files/raisinggradrates.pdf

U.S. Department of Labor, Employment and Training Administration. (2011). *Fastest-growing occupations* [Database]. Retrieved from http://www.careeronestop.org/

Walde, C. A. (2000). *Exemplary tech prep programs combining college connections and work-based learning opportunities* [Report]. Waco, TX: Center for Occupational Research and Development.

CHAPTER 5

Soaring at Full Throttle: Economic Development

Martha M. Ellis

The Challenge:

Meeting business and industry need for workers with in-demand skills for a 21st-century global workforce.

The Response:

GTCC needed only to look in its own backyard to determine that it had an important role to play in supporting the workforce needs of the aviation and transportation industries. GTCC's approach was two-pronged: First, develop new collaborations with industry; second, expand existing programs to support industry needs. GTCC's success in meeting its workforce partners' needs for training skilled workers and bringing new business to the region has attracted funding to sustain these efforts into the future.

College is more valuable to the future economy than petroleum.

— Gregg Easterbrook (2009)

The nation's economy is changing. Much of the traditional manufacturing industry has moved offshore. Partnerships have expanded from the company next door to the business across many miles and often several oceans. As Thomas Friedman (2005) said, "globalization has accidentally made Beijing, Bangalore, and Bethesda next door neighbors." With this globalization has come a new realm of demands for economic development by community college leaders.

Manufacturing that remains in the United States, and in some cases is expanding, is moving to high-tech processes requiring highly skilled technicians. A report in *The New York Times* (Rich, 2010) revealed that a firm seeking to hire employees for new manufacturing jobs was able to find only 47 qualified applicants from a pool of 3,600. Almost one-third of U.S. manufacturing companies that responded to a 2009 survey reported that they are suffering from some level of skills shortage (Deloitte, Oracle, & the Manufacturing Institute, 2009). The demands of staying abreast of changing needs of technology and industry relative to the skills of a future workforce continue to be a top priority for community college leaders.

How do leaders juggle local responsibility and global engagement? Community college leaders are challenged not only with training the future workforce but also with assisting community leaders in attracting new industry. Especially in times of economic downturns, community college leaders often are seen as vital to turning the local economy from recession to prosperity. Colleges have wrestled with the dilemma of how much to proactively reach out across the street and across the world to bring economic development to their regions. Can they risk starting new, untested workforce programs requiring equipment and facilities in tough financial times? Is it really their mission to be catalysts for economic development? Guilford Technical Community College (GTCC) President Donald Cameron believed, "It's our top priority. We really and truly have a vital role to play in economic development" (Kinard, 2008, p. 4).

North Carolina has a rich history of traditional manufacturing, textiles, tobacco, and small farms. The savage ideal that the old way is best and tradition is better than moving forward framed the cultural context that permeated North Carolina when its rich, prosperous history changed course in the late 1990s. North Carolina, much like rural America, the Gulf Coast, and the inner cities, was facing high unemployment with low educational attainment rates. This state that had relied on minimal education for a successful workforce was confronted with a culture of status quo and a failing economy. As President Obama stated, "A good education is no longer a pathway to opportunity; it is a prerequisite" (White House, 2010). If our nation is to stay competitive in a 21st-century economy, the assets of particular regions and states, as well as the nation as a whole, need to be assessed. Industry and community college leaders need to be engaged so that the future workforce can be adequately educated. Partnerships with the global and local corporate community are a necessity. But how are they to be formed and when?

Cameron recognized that GTCC was critical to economic and social transformation in the Piedmont Triad Region (Greensboro, Winston Salem, and High Point), as well as in the state of North Carolina. In 1999–2000 he participated with industry, education, and government leaders in the North Carolina Vision 2030 Project (North Carolina Board of Science and Technology, 2000). The team explored science and technology innovations that would drive the global economy for the next 30 years and developed an inventory of the state's resources in these areas. They developed industry clusters around information technology, biotechnology, and high-tech manufacturing. Biotechnology was selected as the major cluster for the state. The community colleges in the state were crucial to moving this cluster forward and were instructed to develop lab technician programs. While biotechnology was good for some regions of the state, Cameron was convinced that it was not the paramount industry cluster for the Piedmont Triad. He reviewed the significant infrastructure that was already in place to support efforts for economic development and that had career-growth potential.

A RICH HISTORY IN AVIATION

North Carolina's history in aviation began with the notable maiden voyage of the Wright Brothers at Kitty Hawk in 1903. Closer to home, the local airport that is now Piedmont Triad International Airport (PTIA) was founded in 1919. Today, PTIA, a multi-runway, 3,500-acre facility with 50 companies employing over 4,500 people, is a centerpiece for the aviation industry in the southeastern United States. GTCC also has a history of providing an array of aviation training programs, beginning in 1969.

During the 1970s, the Federal Aviation Administration (FAA) approved the airframe and powerplant technician program, and aviation management and career pilot programs were added. These programs developed into the T. H. Davis (founder of Piedmont Airlines and early supporter of the GTCC aviation programs) Aviation Center, located at PTIA. At the Davis Center, students receive hands-on aviation experience, and companies are provided with workers who have received customized, industry-specific training.

When Cameron assessed the strengths of his service area and GTCC, it was apparent that the industry cluster of aviation, transportation, shipping, and logistics was the most promising for the region. In 2005, GTCC and Embry Riddle Aeronautical University (ERAU) signed an articulation agreement through which ERAU would accept all associate degree graduates from GTCC as junior-year students. The students complete the 4-year degree by taking ERAU classes at the Davis Center. This partnership has benefited both institutions. Students seeking an affordable entry into the 4-year aviation degree program begin at GTCC and then complete the program at ERAU. ERAU has seen an increase in university recognition in North Carolina, thereby creating a natural pipeline into both its undergraduate and graduate programs.

For GTCC, the primary ingredients for successful innovation and leveraging of assets included new knowledge development, capable people, and an environment that promotes innovation and entrepreneurship (Rising Above the Gathering Storm Committee, 2010). Ed Frye, chair of GTCC's transportation division, had the knowledge, leadership, and aviation experience to take the aviation program to new heights. A former U.S. Air Force helicopter pilot with 26 years in the Air Force and 13 years instructional experience at GTCC, Frye brought expertise and leadership to providing critical support for expanding aviation's important position in the local, regional, and state economy. Cameron went to work developing a creative economic development ecosystem. The components employed at GTCC for fostering economic and social transformation included nurturing a culture of innovation; securing funding to support new programs; and knowing when to be patient, when to walk away, and when to move forward.

A CULTURE OF INNOVATION FOR NEW COLLABORATIONS AND EXPANSION

GTCC is known for the model workforce development programs created beginning in the 1990s (Kinard, 2008, p. 342). The programs are based on collaboration between business and education leaders. Two questions arise: How can these collaborations be developed? Once developed, how do the strategies become reality? Business leaders and faculty offered answers to these questions. Frye explained that Cameron did not say "no" to exploring new program ideas; rather, he created a culture in which ideas are supported and failure is tolerated, a culture that allows creativity to flow freely. This culture of support for creativity and permission to take calculated risks permeated the college. Cameron relied on content experts, not only to implement the vision but also to help develop it. Therefore, Frye and others had the freedom to try different ideas to meet the needs of the transportation industry and the future workforce.

Developing New Collaborations

Pat Danahy (2009), president of Greensboro Partnership, observed: "The fundamental thing that GTCC does extraordinarily well is that the staff… has a wide interface with the business community and gets feedback on what skills are needed, where our economy is going and where we need to be positioned in terms of programs, curriculum, and so forth, in order to provide the workforce."

The GTCC leaders also have demonstrated poise and subtlety at times when it was needed, as in the early stages of a partnership with Honda. In the 1990s, Honda had a location in a windowless building at PTIA where 60–70 people, mostly engineers from Japan, were employed. In 1999, Honda approached GTCC to borrow several very specific aviation parts, for reasons unknown to GTCC administrators. Frye and Cameron perceived that the Honda representatives would not appreciate being asked too many questions, so they agreed to hold their questions and wait until the reasons were offered. When Honda requested components and GTCC had them available, GTCC loaned them without question.

Years later, the Honda site became Honda Aircraft Company, Inc. (HACI), a global company established to build a new and unique lightweight class of aircraft. HACI entered into a formal partnership with GTCC in 2007, through which GTCC provides training and education for future employees of this light-jet manufacturing company.

In 2008, the first group of 22 production associates entered training for a full FAA airframe and powerplant certificate. Over the next 10 months, subsequent classes began, eventually training 180 future production specialists for Honda. Class start dates were staggered, which allowed different training program completion times to coincide with HACI's planned workforce hiring timeline.

HACI considers GTCC a major partner and a contributing factor in the company's selection of the PTIA location for its world headquarters and light-jet manufacturing plant. Bonita Wellington, human resources manager for HACI, said that while HACI was considering numerous sites around the country, GTCC representatives met with company executives to convince them that the college could provide workforce training for their company's needs. Six months later, GTCC was offering the curriculum with full FAA approval. Cameron's leadership was noted for steering GTCC as a vessel of economic development for the community. Wellington said:

> GTCC's program is outstanding, from their instructors to their administrative people. The caliber of graduates has been excellent. They will tell us they will do whatever it takes to achieve what we need of them; and in the business world, that is what you need to hear. GTCC provides a quick turnaround; their response time is lightning speed, and it is very uncommon to find that." (personal communication, August 19, 2010)

A very different type of new collaboration for the industry cluster is a Piedmont Triad–wide articulation program for supply chain, logistics, and transportation management (SCLTM) education. The University of North Carolina–Greensboro Bryan School of Business and Economics and GTCC were awarded a research grant by the Piedmont Triad Partnership to develop a Virtual Regional Campus for SCLTM education. A team comprising representatives from community colleges, public and private 4-year academic institutions, and SCLTM private-sector professionals conducted the research to identify current SCLTM course offerings in the Piedmont Triad Region, other North Carolina institutions, and nationally respected leaders in the field such as University of Memphis and Georgia Institute of Technology. Faculty from educational institutions, along with business representatives, took the research findings and carefully developed a set of four core courses that would provide students with the skills they would need to enter or advance in the SCTLM field. Upon successful completion of the four courses, students qualify for a certificate of career readiness in SCLTM issued by the North Carolina Center for Global Logistics.

The team also developed an articulation agreement for these courses with the participating educational institutions. Students are able to take the courses at any of the participating institutions and apply the credit toward a 2- or 4-year degree. Articulation agreements benefit these institutions because they can offer an expanded curriculum without expending resources. Seven Piedmont Triad institutions of higher learning chose to participate in the Virtual Campus, which ensures efficient utilization of scarce instructional resources while fostering comprehensive economic development for the region.

This partnership and the North Carolina Center for Global Logistics will position the Piedmont Triad as the premier center for global logistics on the eastern seaboard. Drawing from the expertise of the participating educational institutions, the center will provide additional resources to enhance the operations of the major existing business clusters in the region. The center also will assist economic developers in recruiting new business and industry to the Piedmont Triad. Key to the success of this model is that information from all of the colleges and universities will be available under one roof— at a regional location at GTCC's Donald W. Cameron Campus (Northwest Campus). (See Piedmont Triad Partnership, 2011, for a list of the institutions and industry collaborators.)

Expanding Existing Programs

Triad International Maintenance Company (TIMCO) is the largest independent third-party aircraft maintenance and repair and overhaul provider in the United States. TIMCO has 16 hangars for overhaul and repair of aircraft, with 4 of these hangars and 1,675 employees at PTIA. GTCC and TIMCO have been partners for more than 20 years. Kip Blakely, vice president of sales and marketing for TIMCO, spoke of the innovations in his company and at GTCC:

We are in a new era here at TIMCO. We want to build the hangar of the future. The future is sustainability and high-tech interior designs and materials. There are proactive needs of new aircraft that have to be addressed. We need 400–500 people to make that happen. GTCC can make that happen for us. (personal communication, August 19, 2010)

In an interview with *Aviation Today* (2010), Ron Utecht, co-CEO of TIMCO, and Don Kirkman, president and CEO of the Piedmont Triad Partnership, noted GTCC's role as a key partner in ensuring the local workforce remains strong and well qualified. Utecht said of GTCC's leaders, "they are not only supportive, they are proactive." Kirkman said the industry is always changing in a global market and needs "access to talent" to be competitive, and that the workforce in the area is committed and has the "willingness to embrace continuous improvement." The industry's ability to grow depends on a good employee base, and sharing people and creating synergy promotes higher skill levels among all of the industries at PTIA. They emphasized that the support of the local community and the quality of workforce were vital. They valued that GTCC educates hometown people who stay in the area after completing their training, and that GTCC proactively makes proposals in expanding the joint work of preparing a quality workforce.

Next Steps

Expanding and maintaining existing partnerships, as well as developing new partnerships, are ongoing, continuing processes. Economic development through innovation, relationship-building activities, and leveraging resources is paramount in promoting a new and expanding industry opportunity for a region. At GTCC, fence-line companies and support systems continue to be explored, including a simulation company for the Honda Jet. This company would certify pilots for the new light jet. New types of jets require new types of training for pilots and implementation of new safety requirements. Recognizing this need, GTCC is working with a variety of entities to develop a flight safety hub to provide training, testing, and certifications for the industry.

Another goal is to continue to attract other aviation manufacturing businesses to PTIA. Each job that is created in the chain of manufacturing activity will generate, on average, another 2.5 jobs in such unrelated endeavors as restaurants, grocery stores, banks, and barber shops (Bivens, 2003). Research on the new manufacturing industry shows that a skilled workforce is the critical key to attracting a diversity of new endeavors. GTCC is committed to this goal, by providing training programs and facilities. When the new GTCC facility at PTIA is complete, the college will have no less than 142,000 square feet of space devoted to aviation programs.

SECURING FUNDING

What president, vice president, or dean has not been approached with a great new idea only to face the challenging reality of how that great idea might be funded? The question that always arises when new collaborations and programs are proposed is how to pay for the buildings, equipment, and faculty to get the program off the ground. The goal for any new programs is to be self-sustaining. However, the first few years require additional resources, as little revenue is generated early in the effort. So the questions arise: Do you take a leap of faith that enrollment will sustain the program? Do you risk moving forward cautiously and slowly for financial concerns while perhaps missing an opportunity? Do you look for partnerships with a variety of stakeholders to assist with the start-up expenses?

Like many colleges, GTCC uses a variety of alternative revenue streams, including bond packages, federal and state grants, and donations from business and industry. The major element to funding success for these very expensive aviation programs is the systemic approach of coupling funding types. Involving all stakeholders in assisting with the acquisition of funding is a concept worthy of attention.

Typically, buildings are funded by referendum bonds that have been approved by voters. GTCC has never lost a bond election. In 2004, a referendum was presented to the fiscally conservative voters of Guilford County; it included funding for an aviation/transportation building. The college involved the county commissioners early in the process. The commissioners supported the concept, based on the fact that GTCC was an economic driver and that the proposed facilities were critical to the institution's ability to train the county's workforce successfully.

Local media endorsed the GTCC bond as a wise investment in the community's future and donated 30-second commercials promoting the proposal. College leaders spent considerable time in the community, explaining how the money from the bond would be used to support economic development for the county. The $47 million bond passed with 63% voter approval and provided $3.5 million for one building.

Through formal and informal collaborations, investing in the college and community provides funds for important workforce-in-training programs. These programs provide opportunities for people who are unemployed or underemployed as a result of many plant closings in the region. For new companies coming to the state, North Carolina provides seed dollars to community colleges to support development and delivery of workforce training programs to address many of their needs. These programs then are offered through continuing education at the college to provide for sustainability of the training programs. The TIMCO partnership began in this manner in 1991.

GTCC's Business Center received a federal grant through the Workforce Innovation in Regional Economic Development (WIRED) program. These funds were used to purchase a variety of top training programs designed to support the region's transportation and logistics economic cluster. The CEOs of TIMCO, Triumph, Honda, and GTCC worked together to secure grant funding. Grants totaling $3.9 million have funded the acquisition of the facilities and equipment, curriculum development, and faculty professional education to meet the training requirements of GTCC's aviation industry partners. The Joseph M. Bryan Foundation provided $1 million in 2007 to purchase equipment for structures, avionics, and composites training facilities. Support for the grant was spurred by HACI's announcement that it would locate its world headquarters, as well as research and development and manufacturing facilities, at PTIA. Duke Energy followed with a grant in 2008, to assist in the development of an avionics program. The program currently has the capacity to graduate 36–40 avionics technicians annually.

The next year, the Golden LEAF Foundation provided GTCC and its partners (North Carolina A&T University, Forsyth County School System, and the Greensboro Workforce Development Board) with a $1.45 million grant with which GTCC could develop a sustainable pipeline of trained employees for the aviation industry in the Piedmont Triad and the state. This grant allows for equipping a newly developed program in nondestructive inspections as well as an aircraft interiors and aircraft painting program. All three of these grants were responses to the needs of Triad aviation industry partners, as identified in the responses to questions asked in a skills gap survey.

The aviation industry has donated equipment to the GTCC programs. Greensboro's Cessna Citation Service Center regularly donates aviation parts to the college to augment hands-on student training experiences. TIMCO donated equipment when it needed a new structures technician-training program on very short notice; GTCC utilized experienced TIMCO personnel as adjunct faculty to teach the courses. These courses were offered as a 330-hour continuing education course, and TIMCO paid the fees for training.

Knowing When to Walk Away

Partnerships may take many years to develop. Having the patience and perseverance to stay the course is key to developing and expanding partnerships. Not every partnership with industry will be successful. John Deere came to GTCC to explore the idea of establishing an agricultural technology program. The college and the company tried to implement the training program over a 5-year period, but program enrollment never met expectations and remained extremely small. With such low enrollment, coupled with an expectation from John Deere representatives that the college would provide a building for the training program more quickly than the college could deliver, it became apparent that the partnership was not going to work for either party. Walking away was viewed as a quality decision by both the college and the company.

Another example involved an opportunity with a Chinese aircraft maintenance company that wanted to send 1,000 trainees for training at GTCC over a 10-year period. After discussions, it was clear that this company was positioning itself as an offshore competitor for existing TIMCO customers. A partnership between

GTCC and the Chinese company would have increased enrollment at GTCC significantly, but working with the Chinese company would likely jeopardize the long, successful partnership between GTCC and TIMCO. GTCC respectfully declined the collaboration.

LESSONS LEARNED

- Content experts should be involved in the discussions. Include content expert faculty in discussions with business representatives—and listen to them. Attitude matters. Believe that it can work and that you can do it. Establishing goals and building in the flexibility to alter timelines and procedures are important to success.
- Do not say "no" to program ideas. Do your homework to decide about the most strategic ideas to implement. Create an environment where people are free to try new ideas. As college leader, do not be concerned about getting credit for success. The key is providing the environment for success both inside and outside the college.
- Do not be afraid of failure. Tolerate failures by others. Empower people to create and implement by supporting them in success and failure. Celebrate the successes, and learn from the failures.
- Form partnerships. Partnerships most often begin with informal conversations. All social interactions by the college president should be approached with the intention of mentioning the college as a player. All interactions need to be intentional. Ask companies what they do, and inquire about their vision and goals. Be proactive in arranging informal and formal interactions with CEOs. Do not be afraid to ask about and explore all options. Have patience in developing partnerships, but be ready to implement strategies and programs immediately.
- Positive relationships are critical to success. Relationships are paramount to successful economic development.
- Knowing when to be patient and when to walk away are vital elements in long-term success. Walking away from a potential—or even emerging—collaboration that threatens current positive relationships is in the best interest of the college, the business, and the community.
- Transformation takes commitment. A president needs to give his or her personal time and resources to the community. Serving the needs of the community is an integral part of serving the college. Being a part of the economic and social transformation of the community requires that the president be a central part of initiatives that support that economic and social transformation within the community beyond the college.

REFERENCES

Aviation Today. (2010, June 7). The Piedmont Triad: Incubator for aviation innovation and growth [Podcast]. Retrieved from http://www.aviationtoday.com/podcasts/

Bivens, J. (2003, August). *Updated employment multiplies for U.S. economy* [Working paper]. Retrieved from http://www.epi.org/page1-1old/workingpapers/epi_up_268.pdf

Deloitte Consulting, Oracle Corporation, and the Manufacturing Institute. (2009). *People and profitability: A time of change.* Retrieved from http://www.areadevelopment.com/article_pdf/id45626_skilled-manufacturing-workers.pdf

Easterbrook, G. (2009). *Sonic boom: Globalization at mach speed.* New York, NY: Random House.

Friedman, T. L. (2005). *The world is flat: A brief history of the twenty-first century.* New York, NY: Farrar, Straus, and Giroux.

Kinard Jr., L. W. (2008*). Guilford technical community college 1958-2008: Creating entrepreneurial partnerships for workforce preparedness.* Durham, NC: Carolina Academic Press.

Kinard Jr., L. W. (April 2008). *GTCC's 50th anniversary report to the people.* Greensboro, N.C.: Guilford Technical Community College.

North Carolina Board of Science and Technology. (2000, June). *Vision 2030: Mapping the vision.* Available from http://www.nccommerce.com/scitech/resources/strategic-reports

Piedmont Triad Partnership. (2011). *North Carolina Center for Global Logistics.* Retrieved from http://www.piedmonttriadaerotropolis.com/cgl/

Rich, M. (2010, July 1). Factory jobs return, but employers find skills shortage, *The New York Times.*

Rising Above the Gathering Storm Committee. (2010). *Rising above the gathering storm, revisited: Rapidly approaching Category 5.* Washington, DC: The National Academies Press. Retrieved from http://www.nap.edu/catalog.php?record_id=12999

White House. (2010, August 9). *Remarks by the president on higher education and the economy at the University of Texas at Austin.* Retrieved from http://www.whitehouse.gov/the-press-office/2010/08/09/remarks-president-higher-education-and-economy-university-texas-austin

CHAPTER 6

Embracing Innovation: The Larry Gatlin School of Entertainment Technology

Melinda M. Valdez-Ellis

The Challenge:
Bringing to fruition an ambitious vision for an innovative, world-class school.

The Response:
Garnering support from a cadre of professionals with the combined skills to realize that vision.

If one advances confidently in the direction of his dreams,

and endeavors to live the life which he has imagined,

he will meet with success unexpected in common hours.

— Henry David Thoreau (1992)

A DREAM IS BORN

As an avid country music fan and educational entrepreneur, Donald Cameron contemplated the idea of opening a country music school at Guilford Technical Community College (GTCC) since shortly after becoming president in 1991. The idea stayed with him throughout the years as he remained devoted to his dream. He drafted letters to famous country music artists Dolly Parton and Loretta Lynn, pitching for program support; however, he found himself unable to mail the letters, as he remained apprehensive about the plausibility of the idea. Channeling the thoughts of Babe Ruth, a star from his own favorite pastime, Cameron decided to "Never let the fear of striking out get in [the] way." Cameron persevered, and in 1998 he had a chance to meet Grammy Award–winning artist Larry Gatlin.

Cameron had approximately one month's notice of Gatlin's appearance in High Point. They were both set to attend a reception at the home of Nido Qubein, president of High Point University. During the time he had to prepare, Cameron found himself anxious about presenting his idea. "I had never met someone of Larry's stature in the music business," he said, "and I felt a bit intimidated. I didn't want him to think it was a dumb idea" (personal communication, October 13, 2010).

In *Zen and the Art of Motorcycle Maintenance,* Robert Pirsig wrote, "A person filled with gumption doesn't sit around dissipating and stewing about things. He's at the front of the train of his own awareness, watching to see what's up the track and meeting it when it comes" (1974, p. 303). Cameron knew he had to take the initiative to meet with Gatlin and be thoroughly prepared to explain his vision during their first meeting.

As it happened, Gatlin welcomed the opportunity to meet Cameron and admits that his interest was piqued during the first minute of their initial conversation. Gatlin said he prides himself on assessing a person's character, and he believed Cameron to be a worthwhile business partner. Gatlin perceived that the school would assist many people with music industry aspirations and more importantly, expose them to a higher education. He wrote, "First of all, he's a nice man and a hard worker. I wanted to think about it so I asked to meet with him the next time I'd be in town … we discussed the idea again (and) I felt it in my heart to agree to do it because I thought about the students and I wanted to give them the opportunity to go to college" (personal communication, August 17, 2010). He agreed to partner with GTCC.

NURTURING PROGRAM DEVELOPMENT

Once the partnership agreement was solidified, Gatlin and Cameron decided to focus on a broader concept than a country music school. Gatlin emphasized the importance of including other aspects of the music industry into the school instead of focusing solely on country music. He explained the relevance of including light and sound technical production, artist management, cosmetology, songwriting, and publishing. Cameron agreed and decided he had the makings of a relevant curriculum for an entertainment technology program. They agreed the school would be named the Larry Gatlin School of Entertainment Technology (LGSET).

Discussions between Cameron and Gatlin about the program's focus created an opportunity to modify and enhance the initial vision for the school. Cameron's vision for the school, first and foremost, was student success. He wanted the program to provide its students with the opportunity to explore their talents and allow them to graduate with the confidence to succeed in the music industry. Gatlin provided the necessary insight to ensure that students' talents and self-confidence bloomed while enrolled in the program. He possesses real-world acuteness when explaining his vision for the program philosophy. "The concept is applied and not focused on theory." Together, they realized that Cameron's original vision could be honed by allowing Gatlin's expansive musical entertainment experience to inform curriculum planning.

After waiting many years for a launching platform, Cameron did not hesitate to begin work immediately on developing the program curriculum. This was a transitional time in his presidency, as he began to transform his vision for growing buildings and facilities while concurrently developing the Hospitality Center on the Jamestown Campus in 1997. Cameron invited the recommendation of his vice president of instruction for the person who would transcend a curriculum design. Carolyn Schneider, division chair of Arts and Sciences, and Tom Dupree, adjunct in the Learning Resource Center and freelance audiovisual recording engineer, led the curriculum design team. The team conducted research and traveled to three schools— two located in Texas and the other in Tennessee: Austin Community College (ACC) and South Plains College (SPC) in Texas; and Middle Tennessee State University (MTSU).

The programs at each school mirrored the design team's goals for the LGSET program. The team focused its energy on the state-of-the-art program offerings at SPC. After gathering their observations from visiting the three schools, the team was ready to create its new program. Whereas Gatlin offered the expertise of an industry performer and songwriter, the SPC programs provided the model to guide the work. The design team utilized these valuable tools to build a program offering four curriculum options: entertainment management, performance, sound recording, and lighting. Figure 6.1 lists the required common courses for all four curricular options (not including a co-op work experience consisting of 1 lecture hour per week and 10 clinic/co-op hours per week).

A capstone project provides course topics including planning, preparing, and developing a specific entertainment project. Specific skills associated with developing a project include selecting materials, setting up and monitoring budget, and overseeing a complete project. Once they complete the course, students will be able to create an entertainment project such as a compact disc, project portfolio, or a full concert performance. This course equates to 2 hours of lecture and 2 hours of lab/shop per week. Overall, the course is worth 3 credit hours.

Not including the capstone project course, six courses are unique to the program in the common course curriculum for each of the four options:

1. Introduction to Entertainment: Introduces concepts of various technology systems involved with live entertainment events. Students learn how to describe the equipment required for live events, the technical requirements of touring performance events, and about employment in the industry.
2. Live Sound Production I: Introduces technical skills required for live event sound reinforcement. Students learn how to apply the concepts of live sound reinforcement and set up and operate a small- to medium-scale sound system for a live event.
3. Entertainment Promotion: Examines the elements of marketing and promotion as specifically applicable to the entertainment business. Students learn how to create a marketing and promotion campaign.
4. Entertainment Law: Provides an introduction to the legal aspects of the entertainment industry. Topics include performance rights, songwriting and personal appearance contracts, copyright law, and trademarks.
5. Concert Lighting I: Introduces the technical aspects of concert lighting to explain color theory and instrumentation and how to properly set up a variety of instruments.
6. Recording Engineering I: Details the operation of an audio recording studio to record, mix, and edit in recording sessions.

In just over a year from his initial meeting with Gatlin, Cameron formally announced that the first LGSET classes would begin fall 2000. The next steps were focused on obtaining official approval at the state level and fostering support at the influential community level.

Table 6.1: Required Courses for the Larry Gatlin School of Entertainment Technology	Hours Per Wk		Credit Hrs
Course Title	Lecture	Lab/Shop	
Introduction to Entertainment	2	2	3
Mathematical Models	2	2	3
History of Rock & Roll	3	0	3
Introduction to Computers	1	2	2
Entertainment Law	3	0	3
Live Sound Production I	1	4	3
Fundamentals of Music	3	0	3
Introduction to Communication	3	0	3
Expository Writing	3	0	3
Electronic Music	1	2	2
Professional Writing & Research	3	0	3
General Psychology	3	0	3
Entertainment Promotion	3	0	3
Real Small Business	4	0	4
Work Experience Seminar	1	0	1
Concert Lighting I	2	2	3
Recording Engineering I	2	2	3
Total	36	12	42

VISION IN ACTION

While the process of applying for curriculum approval was initiated with the North Carolina Community College System (NCCCS), program marketing also began soon after the official announcement to introduce the program at GTCC. In early 2000, Lee W. Kinard, then executive assistant to the president, began marketing the program by promoting its existence through written materials, making recruiting visits to high schools, and organizing media coverage opportunities. Kinard provided a spotlight for the program in order to capture the attention of the community. Surveys that were used to gather data on entertainment industry employment trends in the area were rewarded with overwhelming positive feedback for the program—and its future graduates. Approximately 1,000 students were surveyed to determine the feasibility of the program, and over 400 students responded with interest for the school.

An advisory committee was created to discuss program goals, charges of the committee, and how to utilize the observations gathered during the trips to ACC, SPC, and MTSU. The committee members represented a broad cross-section of entertainment industry professionals, recruited actively by Cameron and his team, with expertise in areas such as production, recording, media, and performing (see Table 6.2). While the advisory committee members worked together to learn from each other and advise the GTCC team, the curriculum development committee's focus was on completing its application for NCCCS in March 2000. The short turnaround time of application submission reflected the high level of hard work and time commitment. This illustrates the committee's confidence for the potential of LGSET's success—a testament to Cameron's ability to rally enthusiasm and bring the vision of LGSET to life.

Table 6.2: Members of the Larry Gatlin School of Entertainment Technology Advisory Committee	
Gene Bohi	Retired broadcasting executive
Robin Crowe	Guitarist and owner of Dark Horse Recording Studio
Bill Daves	Local representative of the International Association of Technical State Employees (IATSE)
Ashby Frank	Musician, entertainer, and producer
"Big Paul" Franklin	Piedmont Triad's top country deejay
Thomas Gaffney	Managing Director of the North Carolina Shakespeare Festival, High Point
LaDonna Gatlin	Motivational speaker, singer, and author
Robert Grier	Musician, entertainer, and producer
Claire Holley	Musician, entertainer, and producer
Kristy Jackson	Musician, entertainer, and producer
Cliff Miller	SE System Production Services
Dave Osborne	Owner, Wally West Music Resource
Ed Roberson	American Audio-Video
Kay Saintsing	Executive Director, North Carolina Association of Festivals
Jana Stanfield	Songwriter and performer
Stephanie Wilson	Musician, entertainer, and producer

INDUSTRY EXPERTS ENTER THE CLASSROOM

Cameron turned his attention to securing the LGSET faculty after the NCCCS application was submitted. He knew the program's success largely depended on the strength of the faculty team. A month prior to submitting the application to NCCCS, Kinard joined the GTCC team and the program development committee. Given

Kinard's 43-year career in the media industry, Cameron trusted him to lead the search for the LGSET faculty.

Fresh from his work on the curriculum design team, Tom Dupree was chosen as program coordinator. Thomas "TJ" Johnson also joined the team. Johnson had been living California, where he had enjoyed an almost 20-year career with a varied background in the entertainment industry, but was eager to return to his home state of North Carolina. The third faculty member to join the inaugural LGSET faculty team was Kristy Jackson, who applied for the job of teaching songwriting courses. Already a nationally recognized songwriter and performer, she went on to receive international attention for her song "Little Did She Know She Kissed a Hero," reflecting on the events of September 11, 2001.

The faculty would require the tools and equipment they were accustomed to working with in the field. The technology utilized in the entertainment industry would have to be made available to faculty in order for them to teach with a hands-on learning approach effectively. As in all industries, technological innovations are varied, expensive, and frequently enhanced by their developers. Before the entertainment program could begin, the basic needs for the program had to be met while permanent facility and equipment plans were still developing.

The program's temporary home was in the Business Careers Building on the Jamestown campus. This associate of applied science degree program was launched in August 2000 and was the first entertainment technology program offered in North Carolina. The program started with 80 students, who enjoyed $250,000 worth of recording studios, classrooms, and an auditorium with a proscenium stage. Cameron had succeeded in seeing the program through to fruition. The program was up and running steady at full speed. His complete attention could now center on funding, building, and opening the permanent facility that would house LGSET.

ALL THE BELLS AND WHISTLES

Upon hearing how impressed the curriculum development committee had been with the SPC program, Cameron visited the school with Kinard in early 2000. During this trip he realized the full extent of the equipment and facility requirements needed for optimum program performance. The costs associated with obtaining and housing the expensive equipment was a top planning priority.

The passage of a GTCC bond referendum in May 2000 provided the school with $25 million, with $9.25 million of the total amount designated for LGSET. The decision to build the new school on the High Point campus was an issue of timing, according to Cameron: "We were excited to name the new school as the signature program of the campus, and everything fell into place once we decided to make High Point the new home of the LGSET" (personal communication, October 13, 2010).

GTCC hired a local architectural and design group, Hayes Howell Architects, to design the building and acoustics. The plans called for several state-of-the-art facilities, including the following:

- An outdoor amphitheater with two lighting towers, which would accommodate 600 people.
- A community room adjacent to the amphitheater.
- A indoor sound studio accommodating 225 people.
- A green room with a kitchen.
- Four control rooms with studios.
- Four rehearsal rooms.
- Four music labs.
- One sound lab.
- One lighting lab.
- Numerous offices and classrooms.

As the construction of LGSET neared completion, faculty member Dupree accepted full-time employment with a local theater. Cameron needed to hire a replacement quickly. A national search was launched to fill Dupree's expanded position as the first LGSET department chair. A community member informed a brother of the job announcement. The brother, Jeff Little, was living and working in Nashville at the time and had sought employment with the music programs of several universities. "I had been thinking that I wanted more stability for my family after being on the road in the industry for almost 20 years," he said (personal communication, August 18, 2010). He realized that if he worked for a higher education music program, he could satisfy his need for a change in lifestyle. Little admitted he did not think a 2-year college could offer the music facilities most commonly found at 4-year universities:

It was the first time I thought about working for a two-year college; when I met with Cameron and saw his commitment to the program, I was really impressed. [This job allowed me] to get back to my roots in North Carolina and show my family what it was all about. I thought if I could get this [type of] job, it would allow me to continue doing what I love. (personal communication, August 18, 2010)

For Cameron and the rest of his team, Little's application and subsequent interview was parallel to "angels dropping down from heaven … that's what happened when we hired Jeff Little" (personal communication, August 10, 2010). Little's experience in the entertainment industry was impressive:

- Debuted at age six as a pianist with renowned folk artist Doc Watson.
- Continued in his career 25 years.

- Toured internationally as an accomplished pianist.
- Was an artist manager for musicians John Michael Montgomery and Keith Urban, among others, and for Grammy show productions.
- Managed tours and served as studio musician and sound engineer.
- Received certified platinum records from the Recording Industry Association of America.

A DREAM NO MORE

As the official dedication date approached, it was evident from program enrollment data that student interest had surpassed initial projections. In 3 years, enrollment had nearly tripled. This information provided additional excitement once the 66,000-square-foot LGSET facility opened in January 2004, to serve over 200 students. The effort and dedication put forth by the GTCC team had not been in vain. The program was a success even before it was housed in its own building. The time to celebrate the official dedication arrived on April 28, 2004, as the school's namesake headlined the entertainment performances.

A 4-day celebration was held in honor of the official dedication of the LGSET building. The event was organized to introduce the community to GTCC's newest program and to ascertain the value of a future partnership with the college; therefore, the county's other institutions of higher education were invited to participate in the festivities. Music and entertainment organizations from each of the higher education institutions performed, along with LGSET students and their new department chair. At the dedication, Cameron recognized his LGSET partner by inducting him into the Larry Gatlin School of Entertainment Technology Hall of Fame, as well as two former advisory committee members who had passed away within months of the dedication date: Kay Saintsing and Paul Franklin.

CULTIVATING THE SUCCESS OF A UNIQUE STUDENT POPULATION

A unique student population benefits from the LGSET curriculum. The high percentage of LGSET students from outside the county (60%) results in a positive economic impact to the area, as well as diversity of musical ideas in the classroom. Their endurance and willingness to succeed in the program is evidence of the program's positive reputation.

A creative, comprehensive, and highly specialized curriculum is in place for the LGSET program. Little understands the importance of ensuring that students possess the business knowledge needed to survive in the music industry: Students "need to know about contracts and intellectual property. We focus on a broad set of skill sets because of the convergence of skills needed in this industry" (personal communication, August

18, 2010). Empowering students to learn the business and technical skills to manage their own creative imagination is at the heart of the program. Employing effective instructors to teach these components of the program is the critical piece in place for achieving program goals.

Program faculty members infuse course objectives with inspiration from their own past and share real-world experiences in the music industry. Students are able to benefit from lessons learned by their instructors from as recently as the night before class. Little encourages his faculty to continue their professional musical activities outside the classroom to enhance their teaching effectiveness. Table 6.3 highlights the professional experiences of program faculty. Paired with the required co-op work experience and capstone project, the combination of the LGSET curriculum and instruction is a fortified formula for student success. Little recognizes the importance of his faculty's professional contributions to the program. "They work with a strong advisory committee, network extensively, and maintain (communication) with their industry contacts … our faculty … keep their credentials up to par."

Table 6.3: Professional Experience of Larry Gatlin School of Entertainment Technology Faculty

Instructor	Professional Experience
Thomas Johnson	30-year veteran of the music industry; over 65 worldwide album credits as an engineer, producer, and performer; numerous RIAA gold and platinum albums; member of ASCAP and NARAS; voting member of the Grammy Committee; certified Digidesign ProTools Operator and Reason in The Real World.
Eric Stevie	Bachelor's degree from UNC-Greensboro; owner of lighting design and production company for over five years; lighting and scenic designer; lighting designer electrician; master electrician; moving light programmer; and sound engineer.
Richard Tremmel	Former middle and high school band instructor; faculty member of music at UNC-Greensboro; former manager of a major retail music establishment; MIDI sequencing and electronic music specialist, active bass guitarist in nationally touring rock band, former manager of major music retail store, former freelance musician in Hollywood, CA; Master of Music degree from UNC-Greensboro; and Pro Tools Certified Operator.
Kyle Welch	Live sound engineer for Doc Watson, NC Democrat's State Convention; The East Village Opera Co.; The Machine; Toyz; worked on The Backstreet Boys and Billy Joel/Elton John tours; local theater sound engineer production; recording engineer for the Eastern Music Festival, Steve Lynam, The Miles Blues Band, and The Manhattan Project; professional musician who plays guitar with Jaxon Jill Band; classical and jazz guitar performances; and Digidesign certified Pro Tools Operator (most prevalent software in the industry).

NATIONAL AND INTERNATIONAL RECOGNITION

When other schools called upon LGSET to provide guidance for their program ideas, the GTCC team knew its first taste of recognition had arrived. Representatives from Central Arizona College (CAC), near Phoenix, visited GTCC in 2007. As of 2010, CAC's entertainment industry technology program in the Creative Arts Division offers four tracks to an AAS degree. New Mexico Junior College (NMJC) visited in 2007 and began planning its program.

Gatlin received recognition for providing support and inspiration to students in 2008, when he was honored with the Amado M. Peña, Jr., Journey of Excellence Award by the National Institute for Staff and Organizational Development. In 2009, Gatlin received recognition for his contributions to higher education with the International Leadership Award, by the Chair Academy, a provider of worldwide leadership training for college and university leaders.

FUTURE CONSIDERATIONS

Creative and Performing Arts Entertainment Technology

Little is enthusiastic about the creation of one department to house the drama, music, and entertainment technology programs. It was decided that merging the three programs into one department would allow for more student learning opportunities. In addition, it would create a sharpened focus of applied science programs and college transfer programs to work together for student success.

The drama program is offered as a concentration in general studies for an associate degree in fine arts and operates on the Jamestown campus. Students choose to focus on either acting or technical theater skills. The pre-major music program provides students with a foundation in music theory, music history, and applied music performance skills. The pre-major music program has been operating on the High Point campus since 2009.

The idea to create the Creative and Performing Arts Entertainment Technology Department was announced in early 2011. Members of the three programs worked diligently to identify necessary curriculum modifications. The music and drama programs will transfer from the Jamestown to the High Point campus after construction needs have been met. A center for performing arts is being planned to benefit the drama, music, and entertainment technology programs. The center is in the planning stages with funding, construction, and resource alignment considerations as the top priorities. The goal of the center is to bring visibility to all three programs in one area only, within the Creative and Performing Arts Entertainment Technology Department. The creation of the center will serve to increase the spotlight on the LGSET program and on how it complements its sister programs within the newly formed department.

Multimedia and Musical Theater Options

Due to the convergence of multiple technologies in the music industry, Little is enthusiastic about the prospect of creating a multimedia option as a fifth curriculum choice in the entertainment technology program, recognizing that the skill set needed in the industry with digital technology now includes multitracking for archiving. This requires a divergence of skills for successful delivery in the studio. "A multimedia degree would give a baseline on the divergence of skills required for successful employment in the industry," Little said (personal communication, August 18, 2010).

The idea to bring musical theater as a sixth curriculum choice came partly from Gatlin. He has written and performed musical theater pieces, including on Broadway. Gatlin observed, "When Don spoke to me about the idea for a musical theater program, we—that is, myself, Don, Jeff, and Steve Smith (his guitar player)—decided to travel to all of the area high schools to recruit students and generate interest in the program" (Little, personal communication, August 17, 2010).

———•———

Gatlin has continued to lend his professional services in a variety of roles, including teaching a community songwriting seminar, serving as graduation speaker, and performing in a concert for the foundation. The leaders of LGSET are privy to the incessant technological advancements guiding the direction of the musical industry. Remaining receptive to the advances in technology will allow for continued future growth of the program. The quality and effectiveness of the program will continue to expand as faculty expertise and successful leadership remain in play. LGSET is serving community and industry needs as it remains positioned to be the local and national leader in entertainment technology education. The process of market research via surveys to ascertain entertainment industry employment trends in the community enabled GTCC to ensure it was moving in the direction of continuing to meet the needs of the community and receiving value in return. The ongoing activities of public relations assisted in securing a strong public image for LGSET.

LESSONS LEARNED

- Persist in realizing long-term goals. Focus on and stay confident about original goal(s) while navigating obstacles to achieve them.
- Seek and conquer. Be prepared to seize opportunities and make them happen when presented with favorable circumstances. A person filled with gumption understands his or her own ability to make things happen. Take

risks with the notion that you will make it work. Do your homework by continually researching and preparing for the moment to introduce your ideas. Successful first impressions will encourage others to join in persisted efforts and help you with the work required to follow great ideas.

- Welcome and be open to input from stakeholders, positive or negative. Suggestions for improvement and critiques are valuable tools for refining ideas. Create opportunities for stakeholders to enhance and enrich the development of the original vision, mission, and goals. Use a combination of internal and external expertise and external models. Use college leaders and local industry experts to inform program development. Conduct site visits to formulate program goals based on modified models of success. Ensure that research is performed, and arrange for site visits to collect data. Keep the most pressing needs of your college at the forefront of the final decision-making process.
- Value the role of marketing and public relations to generate community support. Conduct market research in the community to determine trends and needs; build your image and help the community understand your project through public relations campaigns.
- Realize the value of investing in state-of-the-art facilities and current industry technology. Prepare students for the real-time demands of the industry. Find and keep team members whose job it is to monitor new developments in technology and advise the college about its technology needs.

REFERENCES

Pirsig, R. M. (1974). *Zen and the art of motorcycle maintenance*. New York: Morrow.
Thoreau, H. D. (1992). In B. Atkinson, Ed., *Walden and other writings* (p. 303). New York: Modern Library.

CONCLUSION

Living in the Futures We Create

John E. Roueche and Suanne D. Roueche

I f there is value in describing and analyzing how Guilford Technical Community College (GTCC) has achieved its reputation, we trust it is in the knowledge about the unique collection of robust, well-thought-of practices being implemented—practices in leadership, stewardship, partnership, and teaching and learning. These practices thrive in a culture that consistently raises the bar for high performance and achievement standards. Over the course of this effort, we have appreciated and developed an even greater respect for this college that has opened its doors and its soul to our request to look inside at its initiatives, programs, successes, and disappointments—and at the human side of the house.

At the outset of this study, we observed that we could have elected to showcase the work of a number of colleges that have achieved noteworthy reputations for success on multiple fronts. However, we chose to tell the story of GTCC. We made the disclaimer that choosing to study one single college was not to imply it is a "model" institution, but rather that its remarkable history and story deserved telling. The breadth and depth of its successes on more fronts than any colleges we have studied to date have provided us with a rich and fascinating look at a remarkable mix of hard work, good luck, and the fortuity of leadership's sharp insight and strong intuition that has moved its vision for itself into reality for all of its constituents.

As an institution, it is charging forward and well with initiatives that challenge the prevailing theory that community colleges cannot be all things to all people successfully, that they cannot do multiple things well without sacrificing some for others. On a number of fronts, GTCC has reminded us of some of the best colleges we have seen, as they struggle to meet the goals of Achieving the Dream: Community Colleges Count (ATD), to improve student retention and success, to interface with the community, and—in a compelling vernacular—to become the community's "preferred learning provider." Clearly, many other community colleges are working in this fashion to create their own futures with successful programming and policies that maximize the talents of the professionals charged with improving the reality and the reports about their own performances. However, few colleges have achieved such a seamless bonding and a "oneness" with its constituencies and communities as has GTCC. Few have achieved being the "preferred learning provider" in their communities with such an overwhelming level of agreement among multiple constituencies that this is so. The college has earned a strong reputation for balanced attention to the meeting gamut of student, community, and state needs, and to being a partner with multiple other players to change lives significantly.

GTCC leaders repeatedly ask: "Of what value is this college to this community and to this state?" and "What would this community and state look like without us?" These are daring questions. The answers have on occasion put this college, as they would any other, in two seats simultaneously—the driver's seat in the good times and the hot seat when the answers do not live up to the college's or to the public's expectations. Those questions drive multiple programming and policy efforts, all with an eye on significantly improving student performance and completion, and on solidifying the reality that the work of the college is critical to the growth and development of its community and its state.

We knew that GTCC has had the good fortune of having long-time, consistent leadership, and by association, a well-developed culture of pride, achievement, and tenacity around goals of student access and success. We suspected that having sustained leadership and a well-developed culture was a major force in the creation of this apparently unique college. Moreover, we suspected that this college's responses to living in our collective challenging times are testaments to decisions derived from courageous conversations, followed by purposeful and sustained action that, in fact, have shaped and driven its choice and ultimate goal of living in a future of its own design that would best serve itself, its students, its communities, and its state.

Common themes of mission writ large and missions accomplished emerged from GTCC's long history—more than 25 years of institutional need-informed and market-driven efforts—of local, regional, national, and international recognition for model partnerships with industry, well-developed relationships with local public schools as feeders and 4-year institutions as receivers, and friend-raising initiatives for strengthening and diversifying the local economy by providing a well-trained workforce. The array of front-end efforts over the last decade to level the academic playing field for all students made the themes of "missions accomplished" loom even larger. The story of how past is not always prologue for future efforts was ripe for the telling. This was a college committed to changing its culture and its performance—and doing both with true grit.

The "lessons learned" at the conclusion of each chapter are glimpses of the workings of the various college initiatives and programs relative to all student success—a dominant feature and the "engine" that drive the college train; its insistence on consistently and purposefully developing and supporting leadership at every level; its major workforce and economic development initiatives; its P–16 initiatives that put GTCC at the nexus of educational initiatives across the state of North Carolina; and the arts and culture of a region on the national scene, wrapped up and played out in an enormously successful music and performing venue. We often referred to the range of interests that this college defined in its programming—for example, from the Larry Gatlin School of Entertainment Technology to the Transportation and Aviation Partnerships and Training—as the software and the hardware sides of this enterprise. All told, the lessons learned are not totally new, and they are only as good as the quality and tenacity of the efforts to execute them. They are framed with GTCC in mind, as we have recounted the specifics that led to these concluding remarks. But, without doubt, they are the touch points of courageous conversations about how colleges become very good at what they do, how far they have to go to get better, and what efforts they are willing to make to get there. They are the footpaths to creating futures in which colleges can live. We conclude this effort by extrapolating some of the lessons learned into broader contexts.

A documented history of the pathways leaders have taken to effect the impact that the college has made on its internal and external constituents—especially a history about the particulars of why, how, and with what outcomes the critical decisions and turning points were addressed—is an unexpected boon to putting the present into some larger context and worthy of study. As John McWhorter, a linguist at Columbia University, observed, "people should be more aware of path dependence," the notion that "something that seems normal or inevitable today began with a choice that made sense at a particular time in the past, but survived despite the eclipse of the justification for that choice" (cited in Brooks, 2011). Lee W. Kinard's document breathes life into the college's 50 years (1958–2008) and brings the human factor to introspection, to decision making, to the institutional condition that lifts "doing the business of the college" to a more engaging level—that is, makes it as appealing as such a story can be told—and, therefore, make it a good read. Colleges going about the "business of the college" need to put the complexities created by issues and individuals into a context that can be examined by future decision makers and by those who need a broader perspective from which to chart new paths.

Had this document not gone beyond the "annual report" flavor of information relative to board of trustees' decisions, additions of new positions or programs, or revenue collected, to delve into the personalities and the conversations of the individuals driving the college's train, it would not have generated much interest. Many who read it observed that the personalities and the changing times are well defined and described; and that they help arrange the puzzle pieces into an accurate picture of how things were and came to be. Colleges considering their own documentaries should take special note that defining and explaining the "human factors" behind the decisions to take a left or right turn, a detour or a pit stop, will resonate with casual readers and focused researchers.

It all matters, but strong leadership and the culture it spawns and develops matter most. Successful leadership is critical throughout the organization, but it starts at the top with the board and the president, reading from the same pages, speaking with one voice about student success and the transformation of the college. Leadership matters; it is apparent at GTCC in leadership development opportunities. They are strategic, ongoing, and varied. They leave out no one, and they engage them in multiple opportunities to become family, to form cadres of individuals working together on the important business of the college. Having important work to do together is the key to success of embracing goals, reaching benchmarks, and taking care of the work to be done with outcomes that exude college pride in missions accomplished. It is celebrating quality leadership formally and informally with awards, notes, and praise and recognizing the talents of all in the college who contribute to the bottom lines of revenue and success agenda achievements.

What individuals decide to do together determines the behaviors they exhibit, their mind-sets, and their achievements. The culture of the college can either put it in the driver's seat for effecting change or in the passenger seat as change is dictated to it. As Ralph Waldo Emerson observed: "A man is what he is thinking about all day long." Seriously engaged in discussions about student success, the college began working on ATD's goals and objectives long before the grant was written and submitted.

GTCC agreed that the culture of the college had to change in order to effect institutional program and policy changes to improve performance were both necessary and inevitable. Top-level administrators—the president and the board—led the effort deep into and widely across the college. It was their actions that became the models for pursuing the vision of changing the student success landscape, its tone and parameters. The behaviors they exhibited brought faculty and staff to a new awareness that all of them were to be part of the change process, that they were critical to its success, that they would be the beneficiaries of its success and not its victims. They were in charge of the "teachable moments" for administrators and faculty who, understandably, were concerned about loss of power, authority, and job security.

Individuals who are brought into the design and operation of a culture change— whether it is via leadership development or the freedom to experiment programmatically without fear of failure—are those who own it and are more willing to embrace the inevitable critical shifts in perspectives and responsibilities. Colleges have opportunities to grow and develop, to try new ideas, all the time. But they can do so only under the power of the enthusiasm and willingness of individuals who believe that their jobs and their roles in the institution will be secure even as they have the "courageous conversations" that frequently question old practices and simultaneously require, then encourage them to try out and on new ways of doing business (Jenkins, 2008).

At GTCC, faculty are expected, encouraged, and supported to work together within and across discipline areas to achieve improved student outcomes. They are freed up to try new ideas, assess the outcomes, and bring them to the planning tables secure that news will be received in the interest of improving everyone's performance. The college has a genuine and proven interest in a cultural change in which challenges are seen as opportunities, and "driven by embedding high expectations in all things

… the culture creates a climate in which people want to do better and have higher expectations of themselves, holding other accountable to the same standard" (Massey & Hart, 2010, p. 27).

Taking calculated risks is a strategy more likely to be successful and to do less damage if the results are disappointing when taken within a culture sustained by individuals willing to embrace change, the hard work associated with effecting it, and the potential of failure or success; and they are capable of "seeing" the value of taking those risks. Psychologists and neuroscientists, among others in disciplines that study human behavior, describe cultures as emergent systems; in emergent systems, different elements interact to create a new element that is greater than the sum of its respective parts. Cultures are defined as emergent systems, developed by individuals and groups interacting with one another. Group interactions form patterns that influence how individuals in them behave. Brooks (2011) proffered examples of emergent systems include the country's struggling economy, bad marriages, and rising health-care costs. We also recognize that college cultures can be positive emergent systems, or not, and that the patterns of behavior of individuals and groups focused on change define the terms by which they decide to do the work of the college. It is an agreement on the vision and the ground rules relative to the behaviors toward achieving it that creates the critical synergy.

In rallying administrators, faculty, and staff around collective efforts to improve student success—at GTCC, from ATD initiatives, Bill & Melinda Gates Foundation initiatives, to institutional policy and program changes and cutting-edge programming to meet diverse student interests—and moving as a body toward the goals of improving student performance and completion rates, interactions between them while focused on a common goal have created a culture in transition. It has taken time, but it is at developmental stage from which it cannot—would not—retreat.

Stellar leadership demands a fine balance of a healthy dose of respect for the position and the expectation that forward progress is written into the job description, and the willingness of the leader to be a willing and able partner in the work of engineering and bringing to fruition the achievements that support and solidify that respect. Servant leadership is that rare human commodity that appears at the helm and in the trenches simultaneously. It speaks to a willingness to move off the dais and onto the level playing field. It speaks to hard work and the willingness to do it. It addresses the human factor of relationships that take time, money, and effort and that often are the bumps in the night for presidents and leaders at all levels.

Great ideas within the vision are only as good as the leader's abilities to execute them. Successfully moving from "wow" to "how"— from having great ideas and putting them into practice and making them work—is the genius in the enterprise. It is in that execution—that ability to envision, manage, and advance the logistical details that move the idea from a visionary concept to full and practical implementation. While many constituents admired GTCC's president Donald Cameron's ability to get his arms around an initiative, to bring internal and external constituents into the conversation and get them excited about its potential, even more of them admired his ability to see how the initiative could be crafted and brought to fruition. He served as catalyst for the idea and as collaborator when multiple partners were involved. He described the idea in terms that all could understand and to excite them about it in the process.

Becoming more humane organizations can take colleges a long way toward becoming more effective in meeting the demands of the student success and completion agenda. The "humanity" factor at GTCC runs the gamut from the first relationships that students experience with the work of the college—whether they are enrolled in tech prep or early middle college class or walking through the college doors for the first time and without any former experience with the college—to the work ethic of the college's personnel who are focused on making the GTCC experience profitable, productive, and pleasurable. It goes far beyond encouraging students to come in and "try," to wade into unfamiliar territory unattended and uninformed. It thinks through every possibility that might create potential barriers to retention and completion; and it acts to reduce or remove them. It wrestles with the challenges of the current barriers.

Moreover, it recognizes that the college experience is more than a return on financial investment and improved opportunities for increased earning power. There are payoffs that some would refer to as falling within the "priceless" category—for example, being more open-minded; more willing to accept who they are and others, as well; and more likely to vote, volunteer, and live longer and happier lives (Laliberte, 2011). It is in these institutions that students are introduced to options for choosing success over failure. It is that place where students can learn to be self-sufficient and well about themselves. All told, the college experience should be engaging and time well spent. And, perhaps for many, it will be a great (and remarkably pleasant) surprise! Because more than 90% of GTCC graduates remain in GTCC's service areas following graduation, its graduates are the college's best ambassadors for life-changing experiences. They are further reminders that the image of the college as the community's friend and advocate must be consistent in and out of the institution.

The college as nexus is both an intriguing idea and one whose time has come. Whether the college makes the connections, creates the links, and establishes the ties between goals, opportunities, and achievements, or participates as a major player with others to make those activities happen, it is poised at the center of the matter or the situation. When community, workforce, and economic needs arise, it is important that the college is that entity to which constituents look to address them. The college as nexus is a special combination of carefully orchestrated and naturally occurring phenomena. Achieving that status is the result of prolonged, consistent, and successful engineering. As nexus, the college is at its best as servant leader, best friend, and advocate.

Partnerships are powerful combinations; those that align funds with commitment and that align the critical support of dollars where efforts to make a difference reside are the partnerships that confirm belief in possibilities where philosophy is aligned with action. Seed monies can be the fertilizers and gardeners for innovation, and can make the otherwise impossible, possible. In its 5-year summative report of ATD, the Center for Applied Research (2009) identified potential lessons of value for other colleges from the GTCC experience. One of the lessons they identified was that Guilford employees were almost unanimous in their agreement that the ATD grant provided the jump-start the college needed to think out loud and with some assurance that new initiatives and the "unfettered seed money to pursue specific student success objectives" would open doors for the "realization of new ideas for strategies that were previously unfundable" (2009, p. 38).

In 2006, GTCC's vice president of educational support services observed: "The budget comes down to a complex formula which provides a core amount for administration, but if you want to do imaginative things, you have to have outside money to do it" (Center for Applied Research, 2009, p. 37). The critical success of partnerships between this college and economic and workforce development initiatives have become legend in North Carolina, across the nation, and internationally. We contend that another partnership, between GTCC and the Lumina Foundation and Bill & Melinda Gates Foundation, via ATD and Developmental Education Initiatives, realized in their seed money and confidence in the college's ability to generate important change, improve student success, and change the college culture to embrace accountability and improved outcomes, made possible the college's financial commitment to that change. It began with the enthusiasm generated early on by the possibility of grant funds that began engagement and coalition of faculty and staff from the very beginning with what became courageous conversations. The GTCC experience sustains the confidence in the possibilities and successes of individuals who believe in students—all students—working together to combine the power of money and practiced effort, and the extraordinary differences they can make in students' lives and the college's life, as well.

College leaders should decide to live in the future that the college envisions and creates, not the future it would otherwise inherit. Professional strategic planners frequently ask their clients whether they would choose to live in a future that they would *inherit* (if they did nothing), or would choose to live in a future that they could *accept* (a relatively less painful choice among some others with larger downsides), or would choose to live in a future that they could *create* for themselves. GTCC's student welcome mat announces that the college is "Where futures are created!" Many colleges count on their public relations' gurus to bundle hopes and dreams and opportunities into catchy phrases that promise positive changes in individual and collective futures. We learned in this study that GTCC has branded not only its external self, but its internal self, with the idea that futures can be changed and created a new. By helping students create their own futures, GTCC creates a better one for itself. Creating a future in which it can live and work in good conscience that is doing all it can do to accomplish the new student success goals across the institution appears to be the future of choice at GTCC.

REFERENCES

Brooks, D. (2011, March 28). Tools for thinking. *The New York Times*.

Center for Applied Research. (2009, June). *Five-year summative evaluation of the Achieving the Dream initiative for Guilford Technical Community College*. Charlotte, NC: Central Piedmont Community College.

Jenkins, D. (2008). *Lessons: Lumina Foundation report, winter edition*. Indianapolis, IN: Lumina Foundation for Education.

Laliberte, R. (2011, March). Do kids need college? *Family Circle*, pp. 54–60.

Massey, E. R., & Hart, C. T. (2010, Fall/Winter). Realizing potential: It's about the culture. *Community College Entrepreneurship*, pp. 6–7, 26–27.

ABOUT THE AUTHORS

Martha M. Ellis is associate vice chancellor for community college partnerships at the University of Texas (UT) System. Prior to coming to the UT System, Martha had 28 years of experience, including the presidency for two colleges, and various leadership and faculty positions at community colleges, in Texas and New Mexico. Ellis recently served as a commissioner for the Commission on Colleges for the Southern Association of Colleges and Schools, the Commission on Women in Higher Education for the American Council on Education, and the American Association of Community Colleges (AACC) Board of Directors. Ellis coordinates and facilitates the Future Leaders Institute for Workforce Development for AACC. She has received numerous teaching and leadership awards, has written scholarly publications, and is a frequent presenter at national conferences. Ellis has volunteered on various chamber, economic development, and hospital boards.

John E. Roueche is a nationally recognized authority in community college education and the author of 35 books and more than 150 chapters and articles. He serves as president of the Roueche Graduate Center, National American University, in Austin, Texas, after a 42-year career as professor and director of the Community College Leadership Program at The University of Texas at Austin (UT-Austin). He has spoken to more than 1,300 community colleges and universities since 1970. A 1981 study at Florida State University named him outstanding living author in the field of community college education. He received the 1988 B. Lamar Johnson National Distinguished Leadership Award from the League for Innovation in the Community College; the 1986 Distinguished Leadership Award from the American Association of Community Colleges; the 1986 Distinguished Research Publication Award from the National Association of Developmental Education; the 1985 Outstanding Learned Article Award from the United States Press Association; the 1984 Golden Key Distinguished Research Award from UT-Austin; the 1982 Teaching Excellence Award from UT-Austin; and the 1977, 1992, 1993, and 1996 Outstanding Research Awards from the Council of

Universities and Colleges. He was selected by UT-Austin faculty to receive the 1994 Dean's Distinguished Faculty award. In 1998, he was honored by his colleagues with UT-Austin Career Research Excellence Award, the university's highest research prize. Three of his books with Suanne D. Roueche were selected by the Public Broadcasting Service for national broadcasts. He and Suanne received the 2011 O'Banion Award for Leadership in Teaching and Learning.

Suanne D. Roueche is the author of 13 books and more than 35 articles and chapters. She served as director of the National Institute for Staff and Organizational Development (NISOD) for 20 years. She received the 1997 National Leadership Award from the American Association of Community Colleges, the 1984 Outstanding Research Publication Award from the Council of Universities and Colleges, and the 1987–1988 Distinguished Research/Writing Award from the National Council of Staff and Program Development, and she shared with John Roueche the 2011 O'Banion Award for Leadership in Teaching and Learning. She conceptualized and developed the Community College Teaching Internship Program at The University of Texas at Austin (UT-Austin) and organized and developed the first comprehensive developmental studies program at El Centro College, Texas, where she taught for a decade before joining the staff at UT-Austin.

Melinda M. Valdez-Ellis currently serves as associate program director for academic planning and policy in the Deputy Commissioner's Office at the Texas Higher Education Coordinating Board and has recently completed a postdoctoral research fellowship in educational administration at the University of Texas at Austin (UT-Austin), where she completed her doctorate, specializing in community college leadership programs. Valdez-Ellis earlier completed an internship with the U.S. Department of Education in the Office of Vocational and Adult Education, served as an academic advisor at Austin Community College, and was as a graduate research assistant at the Center for Community College Student Engagement at UT-Austin. Her doctoral dissertation examined the role in P–16 programs to identify the elements of student success. Valdez-Ellis has been an award-winning educator for over a decade, holding current certifications in general education, special education, English as a second language, and P–12 principalship. She has presented at numerous education conferences and symposiums for both K–12 and higher education audiences.

INDEX